# THE MILITARY EFFECT

Scott Manthorne

www.atlaselitepublishingpartners.com

**The Military Effect**

ISBN: 978-1-962825-14-6

# CONTENTS

ENDORSEMENTS ............................................................... 5

INTRODUCTION ............................................................... 7

April Shprintz, Air Force ............................................... 9

Blake Hogan, Marines ................................................... 12

Brendan Aronson, Marines ............................................. 16

Brett Whitsitt, Navy ..................................................... 19

Carrie Roeger, Marines ................................................. 22

Christopher William Rohe, Air Force ............................... 25

Clint Musgrove, Army ................................................... 28

Dallas Jamison, Navy .................................................... 31

Dan Jarvis, Army ......................................................... 34

Diana Villa, Army ........................................................ 37

D.J. Vanas, Air Force .................................................... 41

Garth Massey, Marines ................................................. 44

Gene Moran, Navy ....................................................... 47

George Kovatch, Coast Guard ........................................ 51

Heather Throne, Army .................................................. 56

J Scot Heathman, Air Force ........................................... 59

James "Bart" Bartelloni, Navy ........................................ 63

Joe Musselman, Navy ................................................... 67

John Keating, Army ...................................................... 70

Juliana Mercer, Marines ............................................... 73

Juliana Vida, Navy ....................................................... 76

Katherine Rowe, Army .................................................. 79

Kirsten Campbell Brunson, Army .................................... 82

Larisa Harrington, Air Force .......................................... 84

Laura Noel, Air Force 86

Lindsey Streeter, Army 89

Mark Zinno, Army 92

Marlene Andersch, Air Force 95

Matthew Griffin, Army 98

Meaghan Mobbs, Army 101

Micah Niebauer, Army 104

Michelle "Mace" Curran, Air Force 106

Mike Sarraille, Navy 109

Misty Cook, Marines 112

Molly Jenks, Army 116

Neal Conlon, Marines 119

Patrick George, Marines 122

Robert Hamilton Owens, Air Force 125

Sal Filardi, Army 128

Shannon Potts, Marines 131

Stacy Raske, Army 134

Suzanne Lesko, Navy 136

Tameka Rushing, Air Force 139

Tammy Laird, Army/Air Force 142

Tracey Jones, Air Force 145

Travis Mills, Army 148

Tyler Van Hook, Marines 150

Valerie Lavin, Army 153

Vian Morales, Army 157

Victoria Rydin Boncz, Air Force 160

BIOGRAPHIES 163

ACKNOWLEDGEMENTS 194

ABOUT THE AUTHOR 195

# ENDORSEMENTS

What makes military service unique among other career paths? For the longest time, there hasn't been a clear answer. Yet, those who served in the military know there's something different – something special – about their experience.

Scott Manthorne has put a name to this distinctive and defining experience. He calls it *The Military Effect*. From over 50 interviews of women and men who served, he uncovers how their military effect shapes each's journey and their life afterward. Scott also shows how the military effect has immense value in the modern workplace for its foundation of community, camaraderie, and connection.

Yet, what makes this book so compelling are the stories, themselves: The shared experiences of women and men who served, the opportunities and challenges, the lessons learned in becoming who they are today, and how it continues to prepare them for what's next. These stories allow all of us –regardless if one has served or not – to learn from each other, and to see ourselves. I know I did. And for that, this is a must-read.

**Anne Macdonald**
*Brigadier General, U.S. Army, Retired*
*President, United States Army Women's Foundation*

I wholeheartedly recommend Scott Manthorne's *The Military Effect.* This book skillfully weaves together the stories of military veterans who have harnessed their training, discipline, and resilience to overcome challenges and excel in various fields. It beautifully highlights the unique qualities and perspectives that veterans bring to the table.

*The Military Effect* not only showcases the triumphs of these featured veterans but also imparts valuable lessons for anyone striving for success. It serves as a testament to the incredible potential within each veteran and serves as a reminder of the strength derived from their service.

Written in an engaging and compassionate manner, this book is a must-read for those seeking motivation and insight into the power of military service as a foundation for remarkable achievements in civilian life.

**John E. Michel**
*Brig. General, USAF (Ret)*
*Founder, Soulcial Kitchen and the Soulcial Solutions Foundation*

I thoroughly enjoyed reading Scott Manthorne's *The Military Effect.* So many times, I have been asked, "what kept you in the Marine Corps for 35 years?" My answer was always "the people." Scott's collection of stories and service highlights the incredible talent, resilience and creativity available to our nation through the experience and continued service of its Veterans. The book is a treasure trove of encouragement, guidance and hope for our future.

**Lori Reynolds**
*LtGen (ret) USMC*

Impactful and inspiring, *The Military Effect* is an inside look at what life in the military taught 50 veterans and how those lessons set them up for success as they negotiated their next phase in life. Scott Manthorne has done a superb job showcasing these veterans, who each entered the service for different reasons but departed with strikingly similar tales of self-discovery and growth. Each story packs a punch, leaving the reader with actionable lessons about the power of teamwork, tenacity, and honor.

A resource not only for those on the cusp of a life transition, but also for young adults just starting out in life. This book will serve as a source of encouragement, as well as a timely reminder that most growth comes after navigating something difficult, unexpected, or uncomfortable. As these veterans discovered, it is in those moments that you tap into your hidden strengths. The work ethic, determination, and commitment to team that these men and women learned in the military – regardless of how long they served – launched them forward on the paths they chose to walk.

**Patricia Abt George**
*USMA Class of 1988*
*Veteran, Operation Desert Storm*
*M.Ed, Vanderbilt University*
*Daughter, Sibling, Spouse and Mother of a U.S. Army Veteran*

For generations much has been debated about the effects of military service and its benefit to those that have served. In Scott Manthorne 's new book he cleverly dissects the diverse experiences of veterans which have clearly brought added value to individuals, community and our nation. Our communities, businesses and organizational structure have benefited from the discipline, integrity and mission focus that our former warriors bring to any challenge. Scott's work reminds us of the ongoing unanticipated societal benefits of uniformed service. Read it and be proud of our nation's heritage.

**VADM (Ret) Richard Carmona**
*17th Surgeon General of The United States*
*Former US Army Special Forces combat veteran*

# INTRODUCTION

## WHY I WROTE IT

I did not serve, nor do I come from a family that did. But I wanted to do something to say "Thank You" to those that have protected us from harm and given so much of themselves in doing so.

Through the generosity of two good friends (and veterans) and my professional network, I was quickly introduced to those that are featured in *The Military Effect*. In this writing journey I was humbled, I was honored, I was happy, I was emotional and I made fifty new friends. It changed my life, gave me a new community and a purpose in life to serve our veterans.

I will forever be grateful. Each conversation allowed me to learn more about the men & women in our military. I began to understand. And I know that each story you read will be full of impact and value.

## LESSONS LEARNED

- A veteran embodies the best traits. Some of them include commitment, gratitude, honor, respect & service.

- It's a family affair. So much of our military personnel comes from generations of veterans. A sense of duty and pride is passed down from generation to generation.

- Service to our country is not just a tour of duty, or even a career. It's a lifelong commitment to the brothers & sisters each served with.

- Those who choose to serve are our greatest heroes. The sacrifices each make (and continue to) are the foundation for our way of life.

- Veterans are applauded on holidays, and often forgotten otherwise. But their fight never ends, as the memories of service leave oftentimes invisible injuries that never heal. This has to stop!

## THE MILITARY EFFECT

So what lies ahead? Fifty stories of those who served. Each chapter is raw and authentic. Each story is laid out in the same format. The words are theirs, not mine. We worked together as a team to write it.

*About our Participants:*

- 26 men & 24 women. (All but three are veterans. The others are active duty or Reserve, still serving the nation.

- 20 work for or have created their own nonprofits serving the veteran community

- 11 are podcasters, and many more will soon launch their own show

- 14 are authors, who have written more than twenty-five books

## WHAT'S NEXT

My hope is that *The Military Effect* positively impacts every active-duty member and veteran. Serving this community has become my #1 goal. To accomplish this, I have created a program called TME(The Military Effect) Initiative. It will bring together top companies, executives and philanthropists from around the country.

Our goals are simple:

1. Give a book (as a gift) to every military member & veteran who wants one

2. Host networking events with interaction from all business communities

3. Provide training and development on how to better network

4. Recognize authors in each branch by launching a literary award

5. Support companies & achievements with creation of The Disruptor Annual Awards

## WE WILL SUCCEED:

If one veteran learns how to better transition into the civilian work force

If one hiring manager better understands the true capabilities of a veteran looking for work

If one child decides to serve our country

If one of the charities in our stories receives a dollar, or an hour of volunteering

It's our turn to serve.

# 1

# APRIL SHPRINTZ, AIR FORCE

linkedin.com/in/aprilshprintz
**Hometown:** *Soddy Daisy, Tennessee*
**Currently Resides:** *Palm Beach Gardens, Florida*

## WHY I SERVED

In high school, April landed a spot, under early decision, in Boston University's highly competitive broadcasting program under early decision and agreed not to apply to any other schools. Everyone advised against it since paying for college was on her entirely, and she'd be forfeiting other scholarship possibilities.

After the elation of getting accepted, she suffered a crushing blow. She received a partial scholarship, but the remaining annual tuition was several times her full-time salary.

"I burned with shame. Being the first person in my family to go to college was my lifelong dream and, in my eyes, I'd failed. My only option was to take a full-time job and save up to take one course per semester at night at a local college."

That failure turned out to be one of April's greatest blessings.

"My first night school semester, I met a student who'd been in the Air Force. He told me they were paying for him to go to school, which they did for everyone, in addition to paying a salary for the job he did in the military. I remember asking if they had broadcasters and him answering 'only overseas' and jumping out of my seat and telling the professor I had somewhere to be right now!"

It wasn't quite that easy. April went straight to the recruiter's office, but they had never helped a recruit become a military broadcaster – a role that less than 1% of the Air Force performed.

April failed her audition due to bad equipment and only got the courage to try again by helping someone else audition. April then earned a coveted spot as a broadcaster, graduating first in her military broadcasting class.

"We were stationed overseas, covering stories in local communities and on active missions. I lived in Korea and Germany, and I went to places like Afghanistan, Bosnia, & Kosovo to highlight stories of real military heroes."

After her time in the field, April was one of the youngest airmen to earn an anchor position on Air Force Television News, broadcasting to an audience of over 75 million.

## THE TRANSITION

April ended her service after nearly 7 years. "I was at a unique spot where I'd performed every role I could for my rank and age and would have to wait to lead a station. That felt like stagnation. At the same time, there was a drawdown in our career field, where they asked people if they wanted to volunteer to get out early. So, I gave the Air Force two weeks' notice, figuring that's all it would take to find another job".

She was in for a surprise.

"I completely underestimated how difficult it would be to get hired in the corporate world after my service, even with multiple degrees and fantastic skills. It was that experience that led me to open my network to veterans, whether I know them or not, and help them find roles or start and grow their own companies once they get out. I think the one thing the service could do better for our troops is help them learn to network and transition from people who already have."

Once she got her foot in the door in corporate, April was a natural in sales, marketing, and solving problems. Long before it was coined The Generosity Culture[◊], April used her framework of pouring into people, clients and community to become a top 1% salesperson in a muti-billion-dollar company and the top salesperson in a small software start-up that IPO'd for $7 billion just a few years later.

It was a whole new world for April, and she loved it. "I was exceptionally well compensated, and I found so much joy in helping clients, creating processes that made the company better, and mentoring the younger folks." In many ways, it was a preview of what April would do for entrepreneurs and companies with her firm, Driven Outcomes.

It wasn't until April started her company that she really engaged in social media. "I was on LinkedIn when I was in corporate because it was the corporate thing, but I wasn't using any other social media until 2017". Her philosophy is open, connecting with all who reach out. "My network isn't about whether or not people can help me. My network is more about who needs my help. And a lot of times those are folks that I haven't had the pleasure of meeting yet."

In March of 2021, April put that help in an award-winning book, "Magic Blue Rocks, The Secret to Doing Anything" In six short and often funny stories, she lays out a roadmap for success for others with lessons learned from her own mistakes. April says, "How I got into the Air Force is one of the stories. How I managed to get hired in corporate after the Air Force is another. Each story has a principle I learned and how a reader can apply it to their life, to get to success without as many bumps and bruises."

## LESSONS LEARNED

"Military experience gives you the confidence to interact with high-level leaders and the skills to thrive in corporate roles after transitioning out," says April, "I think one of the things that the military really brought out in me was an absolute love for leadership. I don't think there's a better training ground in the world to become a leader."

## WHAT'S NEXT

While running her firm focused on helping entrepreneurs and companies increase revenue through building a culture of generosity, April is on a mission to help people accomplish the impossible. "For me the end game goal is to help as many people as humanly possible." April spreads the word through her Global Top 10 Ranking Podcast, "Winning Mindset Mastery", her book and never being too busy to help.

"I want to impact and help hundreds of millions of people. I will always have time to do that, I'll make time. I meet people where they are and help guide them to exactly where they want to go. Sometimes that's an entrepreneur with a failing company that's been bleeding half a million dollars a year for the past decade that needs me to turn it around and help them sell it for millions. Sometimes it's a company that wants me to do a keynote or a workshop to help their leadership team, or it's a stranger that needs encouragement that they are on the right track in their business, and advice to make it easier. Whatever it is, I'm here for it."

For April, it's not so much a formed idea about what she's going to be and do, it's a formed idea about how many people she's going to help.

## THE MILITARY EFFECT

"The military teaches you things through experience that you're never going to learn through books or teachings because you are able to integrate with the learning through experiences and acting on the knowledge. I think that's something that is often missing in our world today. People amass this great amount of knowledge, but they don't act based on it. And in the military, there's no other way to do it."

# 2

## BLAKE HOGAN, MARINES

linkedin.com/in/blakehogan
**Hometown:** *Blaine, Minnesota*
**Currently Resides:** *Nashville, Tennessee*

## WHY I SERVED

At nine years old, Blake proudly said to his mom, "I'm going to be an officer in the Marine Corps". Growing up without his dad around very much, this desire was fueled by stories of his grandfather. "My granddad was five foot nothing, maybe a hundred pounds. He was a farm boy from northern Minnesota and served as an engineer and diesel mechanic on ships in the European theater." Blake didn't learn until he was older that his dad had been in the Marines, but never deployed. "He actually joined November 10th, 1965. The Marine Corps birthday."

As the time to join came closer, Blake had a stronger urge to play professional hockey as many little kids from Minnesota do. After not making the cut for a Canadian junior hockey team he realized he was overmatched on the ice and that taking pucks to the head as a goalie might not be his best move. "So, I enrolled in the University of Minnesota". Between his junior and senior year, he believed the Marine Corps was the right path but had not been accepted to Officer Candidate School just yet. "My family was telling me you need to go do something different. They were not excited about me joining the Marine Corps. Not many moms want to think about their kids potentially putting themselves in harm's way, but I saw it as if there's something in me. I had that feeling of hearing the sirens and needing to go towards them".

"I ended up going out west for those final summers of college to work on ranches in Colorado and Wyoming reading stacks of books on faith, leadership, and business. One place that left an indelible mark was Lost Creek Ranch, outside of Jackson Hole. At the time, it was owned by one of the original fighting Seabees in the Navy during WWII and he became a mentor to me. I realized then that continuing to pursue a life as a Marine was the right journey for me." After I graduated, I packed a bag for one last adventure to travel around Europe before going to Officer Candidate School. "I made it back to the US with $32 to my name. To prepare for OCS, I was fortunate to live with one of the families I met at Lost Creek who put a roof over my head, taught me about life and business, and even gifted me my first pair of boots to train in. I still have those boots."

Next was a major turning point in his life. "As I prepared to head to OCS, I thought I was going to ship off to war and fight bad guys. And I needed to make it right with my dad." They met on campus at the University of Minnesota. "Dad had been in and out of rehab most of his life and took the bus to meet me. I told him that I wished things had been different, but it was OK, I forgave him, and I love him". Shipping off to training, Blake knew he didn't need his car anymore and gave his dad the keys. "I'll never forget meeting in that little restaurant, and saying to myself, 'Well, that'll be it'."

"At Officer Candidate School (OCS), I started to get letters from my dad. He was trying to sober up. The Marines have a tradition called the First Salute. When you get commissioned, the young officer chooses which enlisted Marine will be their first salute. They present them with a silver dollar solidifying the relationship that the officer's mission is to serve the enlisted Marines."

Blake invited his mom, dad & brother to attend, not knowing who would be able to show up. "Sure enough, my dad was there, and he was sober. He was my first salute and it happened to be on his birthday - August 8th, 2008. I like to think that the Marine Corps played a small role in bringing our family together that day. In fact, the following weekend we were all together in Chicago for my brother's wedding. Those two weekends were really cool moments for us. "

# THE TRANSITION

"At the tail end of The Officer Basic School (TBS), my right foot was not working very well, and neither was my left hip." Blake figured it's just the price your body pays after you've been training so long. "I finally went into medical and asked them to look at my foot. They sent me to Walter Reed for a bone scan and both were pretty beat up." Just like that, his Marine Corps career effectively ended and he entered a medical hold period of diagnoses, surgery, and rehab. "I became a training officer after that and got pretty good at riding a desk and doing lots of paperwork while my fellow Marines went off to their schools and then ultimately go to fight."

"So here I am in Quantico watching the war happen on the news. It took about a year to figure out what's wrong, a year to do surgery, and a year to do rehab and go in front of a medical board." Blake tried to fight through it and get back into training. "Ultimately my body wasn't up to the task. So here I am as a first lieutenant, and I end up getting medically retired."

Sitting in the stairwell devastated, he couldn't believe this was how it would end. "I told myself this is not what my time in uniform will be about and somehow, some way I'll figure out how to serve in another way." Soon, things began to progress rapidly. Blake had built a strong network and was moving forward. "I was working for a program called McWar. I think it stood for Marine Corps Warrior Athlete Rehabilitation program." In his job he met Corporal Cory Hixson who signed his paperwork to attend the

Entrepreneurial Bootcamp for Veterans at Syracuse University. "We were doing medical policy, and I found out about this program. Thanks to Cory, I ended up going, and it put me on this path to serve veteran and military spouse entrepreneurs."

"As my time wound down in the Marines, I knew I had to get a job. I do remember one interesting call that led to my first job. I was trying to get an interview booked at a job fair, but they kept saying no because I didn't fit their profile. I told them I was going to show up anyway so you can put my name on the list, or not, I'll be there. I got a slot in their program and met a Navy veteran that was leading a small sales team for a company called Sage Glass, which was a product built in Minnesota, not far from where I grew up. They gave me the job, and I moved to Southern California with a few stock options and an old Buick. I lived on a boat in Redondo Beach for 300 bucks a month."

Blake got married, and moved to Austin, TX. "It's where I found out about Bunker Labs which is an organization that helps veterans and military spouses with their businesses." Started as a nonprofit in 2014 by Todd Connor, a Navy veteran who served on the USS Bunker Hill. "He wanted to get smart people in the room and throw them the keys." He continues, "My brother & Todd's brother knew each other through church. Todd called me and said, 'We are going to launch the next greatest generation, are you in or out?' Like any good Marine, I immediately said yes and asked zero clarifying questions." Bunker Labs recently celebrated their 10th anniversary.

## LESSONS LEARNED

What it comes down to is one word: access. If you have access to the right people, the right resources and the right capital, your chances of being successful are better than if you don't.

## WHAT'S NEXT

Excited for the future, Bunker Las was recently acquired by Syracuse University's D'Aniello Institute for Veterans and Military Families. "IVMF has been a part of my journey since that first program I attended while on active duty and they continued to be a great partner since day one of Bunker Labs. Bringing our missions under one roof made sense because we could both focus on what we are great at and create a Center of Gravity to serve veteran and military spouse entrepreneurs." He continues, "Bunker Labs is great at building the community, creating those entry points, building that camaraderie and showing that the path is possible. We want to be able to serve the whole community in a much bigger way."

Could we see $10 billion in capital access annually in 10 years?

Can we serve 100,000 veterans and spouses annually?

Can we see a million connections made annually?

Can we support the whole citizen, the whole community, the whole cycle of entrepreneurship?

"This is work that I want to be involved in for the rest of my life. That has been our singular goal since the onset, to close the ecosystem access gap so that veterans and military spouses can pursue the American dream."

"We learned a ton during the Bunker Labs journey and most of it comes down to staying rooted in our core values and that it is all about the relationships. And understanding that the leaders' job is to see over the horizon, create a clear path, and get out of the way to empower the team. Or, as Kelly Perdew, Bunker Labs board member and cofounder of Moonshots Capital would say, 'the job of the CEO is vision, budget, team.'"

## THE MILITARY EFFECT

"There's a book called One Bullet Away by Marine Nathaniel Fick. And it's just, you know, we're all sort of like one lightning strike or one getting hit by a bus away."

# 3

## BRENDAN ARONSON, MARINES

linkedin.com/in/brendanaronson
**Hometown:** *Baltimore, Maryland*
**Currently Resides:** *Santa Monica, California*

## WHY I SERVED

Growing up as a kid, Brendan spent many Saturdays doing the same thing. The routine consisted of going to lunch and the bookstore, then seeing a movie. It was like clockwork. "I would make a beeline for the military history section because it was super interesting to me".

Soon after 9/11, Brendan felt a tremendous urge to serve. "I felt like I had something to offer and that it was the right thing to do. I grew up in a pretty patriotic family". Wanting the challenge to prove what he was capable of, Brendan applied to the service academies in his senior year of high school.

"One of the books that was inspiring for me to get into the military was called One Bullet Away by Nathaniel Fick. Nate went to a rival high school, and we are both from Baltimore, He went into the Marine Corps and became an infantry officer, which was a huge inspiration to me".

A strong student, Brendan was quickly accepted into West Point. But a few days before he was supposed to go, The Naval Academy pulled his name off the wait list. "I was probably the last person admitted to my class at Navy and then made the decision to go there because there's just a myriad of different things you can do when you get out of the Naval Academy".

After spending four years in Annapolis, Brendan knew he wanted to be a Marine. "That desire was reinforced during my time at the academy. My brother also joined the Marine Corps when I was in the Navy, and so he kind of paved the path ahead of me, becoming an infantry officer. This supported my desire and motivation to get in."

## THE TRANSITION

Brendan always had his eye on transition. "I just thought that there were interesting opportunities I would like to pursue on the outside. And so, I got to do most of the things I wanted to do in the military. For me, I just wanted to start a new chapter and find another way to contribute and add a new chapter to my life and career. "

One Bullet Away talked about getting your MBA after being in the military. Many mentors also advised me to take this path. "Getting into an MBA program is a great place to transition, it's a natural career pivot point. It helps you build a great network and gives you a basic understanding of business." Brendan applied to a bunch of MBA programs while he was overseas in Iraq and was accepted into Wharton.

Brendan ended up doing an extra year in the Marine Corps, after that, deferring school. "Getting out in March, I had some time to burn before school started. I applied for this internship program at Goldman Sachs in the investment bank and called every veteran I could." His relentless follow-up and preparation for interviews paid off, with Brendan being accepted into the program.

"I had a really valuable experience at Goldman. The people were fun to work with, and I learned a ton." During his first month of business school, Brendan's dad passed away unexpectedly. "We were very, very close. And so that kind of reshaped what I wanted from my life and what kind of career I would have." Having received an offer to work full time at Goldman, Brendan listened to his professors and got his MBA.

Knowing how important networking was, he has harnessed the power of LinkedIn (one of the most important tools for business in social media). "I am trying to be prolific on LinkedIn. I have over 13,000 followers now. It takes consistency and discipline and I love it. It's super fun. And it's given me an opportunity to meet people I never would have imagined meeting."

"Posting regularly on social media actually really helps develop those relationships. And those relationships will feel like they know you after a few months because they see and learn a lot from the content I post. It's been a huge life and career upgrade".

Brendan's company was a "startup" called Paintru which he created with some veterans. They had an artist take photos of clients and recreate them into gifts. Paintru was launched with a small Angel investor who Brendan met while working at a non-profit coming out of the military.

## LESSONS LEARNED

*Interpersonal Skills*

"Being in the military exposed me to such a variety of different folks from diverse backgrounds. In my platoon alone I was in charge of between 40 to 60 soldiers, depending on what kind of operation we were doing. We had a mix of backgrounds like you would not believe. I mean, we had dudes who were getting out of very challenging environments and looking to the military as a steady paycheck and three meals a day. And then other folks who were from very affluent backgrounds who were dramatically smarter than I am, you know. And so, understanding how to deal with and work with people and try and get the best out of them is really important."

## WHAT'S NEXT

Brendan recently founded The Military Veteran, which focuses on helping companies hire veterans. They also work with veterans to help them move into better careers. " Our in-person events host executives who come and speak about their careers. They are great for transitioning vets or really any veteran in the first five to ten years of their civilian business careers who want to build a great network."

"Transitioning out of the military, you lose a purpose and a mission. You lose a tribe of peers and mentors who are invested in your success, and then you lose financial stability. We sought to alleviate all three of those problems" Brendan goes on to say, "The thing that I think people overlook is the impact of loss of tribe. Our in-person events just build great connections and great friendships".

His events continue to draw incredible speakers. Some of them have included the CEO of Johnson & Johnson, Larry Skorski, and the chairman and CEO of Electron, Larry Smith. ". We have had great success helping veterans get into executive roles and investor roles. For us as an organization, the mission is important for a couple of reasons. First, the number one predictor of whether a company will hire veterans is the presence of a veteran, all the executive team. being able to help folks get into those roles, Second, veterans are really, really underrepresented in investor roles".

Always learning, always adapting, always delivering. Brendan continues to strive for success.

## THE MILITARY EFFECT

"JPMorgan has a great veteran's program. In addition to their hiring programs, they have this mentorship program that is very deliberately run, where they'll pair a veteran with a more senior person at the firm, and that person is either a veteran or a non-veteran". Says Brendan, "The firm found that it's obviously great for the veterans, getting mentorship and being able to understand how to navigate a group as it is different than in the military, which is much more linear. But it's also great for the mentor, especially if that mentor is not a veteran, then they're able to understand what unique challenges veterans face".

# 4

# BRETT WHITSITT, NAVY

linkedin.com/in/brett-whitsitt-9466551b
**Hometown:** *Washington, D.C.*
**Currently Resides:** *New York City, New York*

## WHY I SERVED

Growing up in Virginia, Brett attended the Virginia Military Institute, primarily to play lacrosse. Studying abroad during sophomore year, he met a Naval Academy graduate that was about to start SEAL training. "I just asked him to educate me a little bit on what the application process looks like." It was not long after 9/11, and Brett knew he needed to start thinking about what life would look like after school.

In 2006, Brett applied for a Navy scholarship. "A number of my friends enlisted in the military right after high school and had been on multiple deployments to Iraq. I felt a call to serve, knowing some of my best friends were in harm's way. I wanted to be able to contribute on a broader scale." He immediately started training hard and two years later got picked up into the SEAL program.

"I decided that I wanted to be in a position at the tip of the spear and to contribute in the most meaningful way that I could." Brett concluded that the SEAL teams would be an effective way to do that. "Just preparing to meet the basic minimum standards, even physically, could not be achieved without a lot of very intentional training. So, I took two years of one-on-one swim lessons just to get myself at a passing rate. Understanding it was not the type of challenge that I could take lightly, I went into it with the mentality that I'll die before I quit."

Brett spent the majority of his time with SEAL Team Seven. "They were right in line for heavy deployment cycles, and I did four in the Middle East including two deployments to Afghanistan and one to Iraq. " Throughout his tours, Brett had some excellent mentorship and was given the opportunity for an early promotion to a Platoon Commander assignment at Team Seven. Thereafter, Brett spent two years in Europe involving broader security cooperation, training, and engagement with allies across the region.

## THE TRANSITION

Earlier in his career, Brett had hoped to elevate his status within the SEAL community but, in 2015 after his fourth deployment, decided to explore the business world. "I wanted to go back to grad school with an MBA program being my top priority." His goal was to enter a top-notch MBA program and be able to work full-time, avoiding having to live on Spaghetti-Os for two years. "I always thought that finance was a natural fit for me. It aligned with my undergraduate studies in economics and business with a concentration in financial management."

Soon, he ended up securing a position with JP Morgan in their investment bank and the Leverage Finance Group. Brett was simultaneously doing Wharton's MBA program for executives. "In some ways, I was playing catch up from the previous eight years of being deployed around the globe and climbing over mountains non-stop. I still had to cut my teeth in the business space."

Before the end of the school program, receiving encouragement from his mentors and professors, Brett was on his way to becoming an entrepreneur. "I was a little surprised. I hadn't really considered launching my own business until then, and once again started doing research into another potential endeavor, asking myself what it would entail. Then the light bulb went off and I said, wait a second, no one's built a Siri-like or Jarvis-like capability for the battlefield yet." He then took the plunge, and Squire was born.

"Having been a Ground Forces Commander during hundreds of SEAL missions, I knew exactly where this could go in terms of a new technology solution to streamline communications and collaboration, particularly in time-sensitive scenarios. Whether that's a hostage rescue overseas or even something that is similarly time-sensitive, dealing with a lot of the same issues regarding information flow, for example, in an active shooter scenario for domestic law enforcement response."

With this new illumination, Squire was up and running. The pathway for execution became very, very clear. Building upon a strong foundation with respect to domain experience, in addition to a strong network of friends and colleagues still in uniform, the pathway to new business opportunities was seemingly endless in terms of new technology innovation and getting better tools to our front lines."

## LESSONS LEARNED

"One thing we learned in the SEAL teams was just this spirit of continuous self-improvement, and one of the ways that that was communicated to me was that you should constantly be trying to identify opportunities. This comes through self-awareness. Saying to yourself, 'What are my greatest weaknesses? How can I pour my energy into making those things perhaps my greatest strengths? And then repeat the exercise... Now I'm going to make an intentional effort to make *that weakness* one of my key strengths and then continue the loop and just continue to reiterate."

## WHAT'S NEXT

Slowly but surely, Brett is growing not one, but two companies. "It's a step-by-step process to get stronger. We're about five and a half years into both." One company focuses on voice technology. "It's a really hot segment with the advent of platforms like Siri and Alexa. Voice seemed to be spreading like wildfire and I thought in terms of technology strategy, it could be a really interesting segment to dive into. I'm also very passionate about the second company, which I co-founded with one of my best friends from back home. We have a small business that is primarily focused on facility renovation, maintenance, and specialty service support at healthcare facilities and medical centers for veterans."

"Regarding Squire Solutions, admittedly it's my way to get back and fight. From the outset my view was, if we can get better communication and collaboration tools using technology out in the field to our frontline operators, whether that's soldiers or emergency responders or what have you, and in doing so we can get better actionable information where it needs to go in some of these time sensitive situations, I am of firm belief that's going to save lives on our front lines. My goal is hopefully to contribute to the community in ways that are far greater than anything I might have been able to accomplish by remaining in uniform."

"Both my experience and my network have helped to shape the vision and what we're building. Many people along the way have been able to help me or help the company to navigate where there might be opportunities for deeper traction, and we are gaining additional exposure for our technology in ways that are pretty meaningful as it relates to capability gaps on the battlefield that exist today."

Brett views his position in a leadership role to serve others, to be a resource provider, to be a coach, a mentor and really help others, placing their needs above his own. "I certainly wouldn't be where I am today if I didn't have a long list of people that were helping the coach and guide me along the way."

## THE MILITARY EFFECT

"People certainly are grateful and appreciative of your service. Absolutely, no doubt. And that can do a lot of things... That can get your foot in the door for an interview, for networking or connections, etc. but you still have to prove yourself and pay your dues all over again."

# 5

## CARRIE ROEGER, MARINES

linkedin.com/in/carrieroeger
**Hometown:** *Rhinelander, Wisconsin*
**Currently Resides:** *Marietta, Georgia*

### WHY I SERVED

Carrie didn't know what she wanted to do with her life. "Growing up in a small town in Northern Wisconsin, I watched my mom and dad struggle to put my brother through college and thought, that doesn't make sense for me right now. Why would I spend their money if I don't know what I want to do with my life?" She found an alternate path through the military. "A friend and I went to meet with the Navy recruiter together, she bailed on me – and so did the Navy! The Marine recruiter was there, and within the hour, I was signing up to be a Marine!"

Faced with options and opportunities through good test scores, Carrie chose to pursue a military intelligence career as a Russian Linguist. "My dad was an army veteran in intel as well, so it felt good to follow in his footsteps." The Russian language school was in Monterey Bay, California. "We were in school for a year, so I had plenty of time to explore the California coast. It was amazing!"

From California, Carrie was sent to Texas for additional training. "When we settled in at San Angelo AFB, I discovered I may have joined the wrong service! Our accommodations included a private room, television, microwave, and maid service; nothing I had yet experienced as a Marine!" With school taking well over a year, Carrie's enlistment was a 5-year contract, giving her plenty of time to serve in the fleet at Camp Lejeune, NC.

"Camp Lejeune wasn't exactly amazing, but it was right on the beach, and it was where I was going to play out the rest of my military career. There were a few deployments and some great opportunities for adventure, so it wasn't too bad."

During Desert Shield/Desert Storm, Carrie remained at her unit in Camp Lejeune. Then the opportunity came for her to attend jump school at Ft. Benning, GA. "Jump school was a great opportunity. Not only was it fun, but it really taught me a lot about myself and overcoming fear." As a member of her unit, in a jump billet, Carrie continued to train as a paratrooper and ultimately earned the Navy/Marine Corps Gold Jump wings – the first Woman Marine to be awarded the wings. "Paving the way for other female Marines to be jump qualified was an honor. At the time, the Marine Corps Orders specifically stated "male Marines" in jump billets. Erasing the gender so every could attend was a proud moment in the Marines for me."

## THE TRANSITION

"When I decided to leave, I had already completed two years of education earning an associate degree." Carrie's plan was to go back to Minnesota, finish college, and live happily ever after. "I didn't like the cold and went back to North Carolina within 6 months." Her (then) boyfriend was still stationed there. She was soon engaged, finished school at the University of Wilmington, and then started to find her way in life.

After a short stint in North Carolina working for a construction company, the couple moved to Atlanta. Carrie continued her career in the industry, eventually landing at Windsong Properties where she worked for 13 years.

"My transition is a really interesting story through a set of circumstances." During a trip to Las Vegas for a conference, Carrie and her husband were introduced to a restaurant called the Leatherneck Club Bar and Galley. "It's January of 2015, and we are sitting in this marine centric club, if you will. It has a bar that maybe seats about twelve, a pool table, and Marine Corps memorabilia all around the walls."

Carrie distinctly remembers that day. "Before I even had a chance to sit down, I had a cold beer in my hand. There was a group of older Marines in their 70's, that were sitting at one of the tables in the other section, planning a big trip to Paris Island. They knew I went there. So immediately, I had a seat at the table, and they asked me questions about Paris Island. I was accepted. I felt like I belonged. I was immediately brought into the fold."

It was a life-changing experience. "When we left there, we dared to say, 'Atlanta needs one of these.' it was never a bucket list item that we wanted to open a restaurant or anything like that."

The couple decided to link arms and make it happen. "We found a location by June and opened Semper Fi Bar & Grille in August. We had no restaurant experience for the entire process." Eight years later, the venture was a success. "It was a huge adventure. I mean, the journey into the restaurant, the only thing I can tell you, it was just divine inspiration."

## LESSONS LEARNED

Flexibility and resiliency - hurry up and wait, then be flexible to change direction, rebound from a failure and move on, quickly.

## WHAT'S NEXT

"Big plans are in the works for the years ahead," says Carrie. "We now franchise because we recognize and have come to understand, the impact that we have on the community, especially with the veterans. We truly believe that what we do is duplicatable, and we felt like the next step in this mission is to teach other people how to do the same thing." The restaurant has become a safe space. "Veterans feel like they fit in, belong and can even tell their stories."

This year, the name of the franchise was changed. "We would run into people downtown who knew of Semper Fi, but didn't come in because maybe they weren't military, some even because they weren't Marines, and that's not at all what we were trying to accomplish." By changing the name to Rally Point Grille, they removed the restrictive assumptions and opened the opportunity up to everyone. The community support has been overwhelming and proof it was the right direction to go.

"I'm shooting for thirty locations in the next five years in the southeast and around the major military installations." To be an owner, you have to be veteran, first responder, or Gold Start Family member. Each location runs off the original business model and the new name, Rally Pointe Grille. "Our first franchise is actually a married veteran couple. He is an Army major, and she's former Navy. When we go to sell a franchise, I'm not looking just for Marines who want to buy a Semper Fi. I can sell the franchise to any veteran because it's veteran neutral."

Carrie and her husband chose the name Rally Point Grille because it doesn't mean anything positive or negative to a civilian. "Rally Point Grill actually does speak to a veteran." The group recently signed a partnership agreement with a nonprofit group called Let's Chow. "They're in the Washington DC area and their purpose is to empower veterans to run a successful food truck. We intend on building this partnership so we can move a veteran through the food truck business and into a brick-and-mortar restaurant." The next step is to gather the capital and the financing needed to support the business model.

## THE MILITARY EFFECT

"When you find a veteran who is a great person, they come with a skill set that they learned in a very micro period of time. In the civilian world, it can sometimes take 12, 14, 16 years to learn the same thing. Coming out of the military, even with only four years of service, a veteran knows more about people, leadership, communication and getting the job done than anybody else at that age that didn't go in the military. They have had more responsibility at their age than any of their civilian counterparts. Don't underestimate their competencies, even if you can't understand the lingo of their job history."

## 6

## CHRISTOPHER WILLIAM ROHE, AIR FORCE

https://www.linkedin.com/in/cwrohe/
**Hometown:** *Wykoff, Minnesota*
**Currently Resides:** *Amelia Island, Florida*

### WHY I SERVED

Born and raised in Southeastern Minnesota, Chris grew up in a small conservative and traditional farming community. "My Father was the President of a local bank, and my mother was a nurse at the Mayo Clinic. My life involved the outdoors, church, school and sports, and due to my performance in school and on the field, I received a nomination from my congressman and an offer from the Air Force Academy to play football." He continues, "My mom initially thought I was crazy to go to a service academy and did everything in her power to convince me to stay near home, but after my recruiting visit and experiencing USAFA firsthand, I was committed and wanted the challenge of a military service academy. Although difficult, I knew it would make me a better man and looked forward to the journey."

Chris knew right away he wanted to serve his country and looked forward to USAFA. "I believed in integrity first, service before self, and excellence in all that we do." The four-year journey was challenging and tested Chris at every turn. He made many close bonds with fellow cadets that last to this day, and his overall performance in athletics, academics, and military placed him as an honors graduate and near the top of his class. Overall, he made an indelible mark while at USAFA and his time there ultimately shaped him as a man, professional, and leader. "Following USAFA, I wanted to compete for some of the elite scholarships in advanced business, leadership, and management degrees to further my study or broaden my horizons; and was fortunate to receive the Alan J. Hook Memorial Scholarship to Harvard's Kennedy School of Government to earn a master's degree in public policy." Chris is still very involved with HKS, serves as the chapter President for North Florida, is a special guest to the Dean's Council and volunteers his time to the school for mentoring and guidance.

"I look at my experience in a military service academy and then the stark contrast to an Ivy league educational environment – knowing that these two drastically different, yet top level educational programs pushed and pulled on me fundamentally challenging me in different ways through drastically differing environments." For Chris, this was the best of both worlds and was an accelerated shaping mechanism for his life as a leader, officer in the Air Force, and executive in the business world.

Chris served over 20 years in both active duty and the reserves as a career acquisition professional on many high level focus and priority programs with assignments at Eglin Air Force Base, Camp Smith, and NORAD NORTHCOM to name a few. His career was marked with pushing the envelope for new, novel, and transformative solutions and creatively understanding the acquisition environment to deliver much needed capabilities to the warfighter - solidified by his commendation and meritorious service medal upon retirement.

## THE TRANSITION

"In early 2005, force shaping was enacted and as a result officers in certain career fields were able to transition active-duty commitment to reserve commitment seamlessly. So, I transitioned to a reserve commitment with the full intention of serving until retirement." Chris did, and in 2020 retired as reservist with two positions: one at the 96th Range Group at Eglin Air Force Base and the other as an additional duty Admission Liaison Officer for the United States Air Force Academy in Florida. "These two assignments and the ability to serve as a reserve officer while having a robust civilian career in the defense industry afforded me the opportunity to transition early (or gradually) and live almost a dual or triple life – and I would not change a thing."

Chris' transition was unique in that he had one foot in the reserves as well as one foot in the civilian world for much of his young professional career. He took leadership roles while in service as a reservist and with Toll Brothers, Lockheed Martin Missiles and Fire Control Systems, President of a National Consortia, and ultimately as a co-founder of two aerospace and defense related companies. Throughout his career Chris "chose to affect change in next generation technologies and acquisition pathways to field these systems."

## LESSONS LEARNED

Civilian life is much different from life in service in a truly critical way. In uniform, you serve with those that have the same core values, ethos, mission sets in life and serve under the same command structure. Integrity, honor, and duty at the foundation. These values must be earned and learned from others through experiences in civilian society.

## WHAT'S NEXT

"I'm doing what I'm doing today because of my military service, my experiences, and the networks I have built throughout my career. Today, we have two companies: Rogue Industries® (www.rogueindu.com), which provides novel solutions in infrastructure, manufacturing, and IT and

GuardianSat™ (www.GSAT.space) which is the patent protected market leader in active space situational awareness for assets In GEO. Says Chris, "Both companies are successful, and we focus on hiring transitioning veterans when able because there's an established level of trust for members who have served and worn the uniform with similar backgrounds and similar experiences. This trust, respect and communication really assist with our current mission sets for both companies."

"Due to my time in service and corporate America, I think that the next stage of growth for the military effect is that we, as a society, must recognize the benefit of a military career as well as the differences and uniqueness of each military career and individual as outlined in these interviews. Society shouldn't take veterans and isolate them as a separate segment of the workforce. Military experiences throughout each branch of service are unique in their own regard and this filter must be more mainstream to allow for a smoother transition."

## THE MILITARY EFFECT

"Once you introduce yourself as a veteran, many times the conversation stops and people may have formed an opinion of you, as opposed to you telling them your attributes based on your military service and unique experience. As a veteran, never forget you have a tremendous skill set, you led a team, you were deployed, you were in challenging environments, you are good under pressure and stress and you were given a lot of responsibility, etc. Take the time to quantify the military effect and your unique experience. Following these principles would positively benefit the transition out of a green collar."

# 7

## CLINT MUSGROVE, ARMY

linkedin.com/in/clint-musgrove-41173923
**Hometown:** *Texarkana, Texas*
**Currently Resides:** *Southlake, Texas*

## WHY I SERVED

Growing up in a small rural town in southern Arkansas, Clint had limited options and a realization that his path would not lead to the outcomes desired. "I needed a shift in perspective to change the trajectory of my life and recognized that a change of scenery was required. I didn't want to end up just stuck in place." He knew additional help would be needed to get out and forge a new path for himself. "Early in high school I recognized the benefits and decided the military was likely my best option."

"The military was on my radar as a way to seek adventure, expand my horizons and get an education. It was something I had always been interested in and was actively considering". During Clint's senior year of High School, 9/11 happened. Motivated by his love of the country, and a desire to serve and give back, he enlisted as a combat medic. "Serving was an honor, and my experiences pushed the boundaries of what I thought I was capable of, bringing out the best version of myself. I was very fortunate to have teammates and mentors who chose to see limitations as opportunities for growth."

As a medic, Clint reveled in his role, and the opportunity to be an integral part of a high-functioning team fueled by his passion for making a meaningful impact. His dedication to providing medical care under pressure showcased not only his expertise, but also his unwavering commitment to the well-being of others. "I thrived in that dynamic environment, where quick thinking and decisive actions were essential." Beyond the challenges, the camaraderie within the team created a bond that went beyond professional duties. Says Clint, "It became a shared journey of resilience and support". His journey as a medic was not just a career, but a calling that allowed him to contribute to something greater than himself, leaving an indelible mark on the lives he touched and the team he served.

## THE TRANSITION

On his second deployment to Iraq, Clint faced severe injuries in a large mine-resistant vehicle rollover. Despite his injuries, Clint was able to provide lifesaving aid to his teammates. "Luckily, everyone survived." The subsequent couple of years were predominantly centered on recovery.

During this period, Clint worked tirelessly to maintain fitness and regain his health. The aftermath involved enduring multiple surgeries, engaging in rigorous physical therapy, and the installation of permanent hardware, ultimately leading to Clint's medical retirement in 2013.

Despite the initial disappointment of not being able to continue his military service, the recovery process gifted Clint a different lens with which to view life. Meeting his amazing wife and starting a family further motivated him to move into this time of transition with an open mind. "I recognized that while you cannot control your circumstances, you can control how you respond." This shift in perspective was critical to the challenging prospect of choosing a path forward."

Clint went back to school with no clear idea of what he wanted to do. "I pursued an education in sports medicine with a minor in chemistry. Given my previous experience, civilian medicine seemed the most logical choice." He found logic and passion don't always intersect, and so upon graduation, he pursued work that could utilize his military training, finding more comparable work in the executive protection industry for a time. "The work life balance was not conducive for prioritizing family. I recognized it was time for a change."

"At the time I felt the squeeze of my military background being condensed into very limited options." Like many veterans, Clint struggled to translate how he could add value to industries he was unfamiliar with. Unsure if it was the right path, he found some middle ground working in government service. "I onboarded with DHS & FEMA, accidentally stumbling into disaster management. It wasn't something that I'd ever considered, but it was an opportunity to grow and serve in a different capacity."

After several years of federal service, Clint has taken part in some of the largest disaster response operations in United States history. Now employed in the private sector, he is dedicated to utilizing his knowledge to promote a posture of preparedness, for the betterment of industries critical to the nation's welfare.

## LESSONS LEARNED

Don't get locked in place, push through the desire to become complacent, to settle. We are often trapped by our own perspective, keep an open mind, embrace change, and if you feel stuck or discouraged remember that growth lies in the unfamiliar. Failure is not the absence of success, but an integral part of it. Don't be the limiting factor or bottleneck of your own story.

## WHAT'S NEXT

Clint has found great satisfaction in solving the complex problems associated with disaster response and recovery operations. His recent transition to the private sector presents him with another avenue for growth in the industry. He aspires to leverage his experience to contribute to the industry's advancement through technology-driven solutions.

Clint has extended his network through platforms like LinkedIn. "My role is not one that is forward facing or reliant on leads, so my primary focus on a platform like LinkedIn is to support and connect others. I'm part of a group called The Outlier Project, which does just that. I'm happy to be included in a group that genuinely wants more for people than from people."

"The world is a big place and you're only limited by imagination. Keep an open mind, put others first, and be a person of integrity. You are just one relationship away from finding the next chapter in your life."

## THE MILITARY EFFECT

Clint recommends the book *Tribe* written by Sebastian Junger. The book explores the idea that in times of adversity, people come together, forming tight-knit communities that provide support and purpose. "It identifies core issues that plague military members after service. "Struggles can obviously be induced by trauma, but the loss of a support network and identity can be crippling, making it extremely difficult to find new purpose."

# 8

# DALLAS JAMISON, NAVY

**Hometown:** *Rock Hill, South Carolina*
**Currently Resides:** *Fort Mill, South Carolina*

## WHY I SERVED

Dallas was born to fly. "As early as I can remember, my uncle would often take me up in his plane." He soon caught the aviation bug. "When I was in high school and wasn't doing school stuff, I worked at the local airport pumping gas and doing minor maintenance and stuff like that". He turned that money into flight lessons, soloed at 16 years old and got his private pilot's license. "I knew I wanted to fly for a living."

While working at the airport, Dallas met a man whose great grandfather was a Four-Star Admiral in the Navy and a graduate of the U.S. Naval Academy. "He kept encouraging me, saying I should apply to the Naval Academy". Dallas knew nothing about the military. None of his family had served. He took the advice, applied, and got accepted. "I really didn't know what I was getting myself into. I just went online and started the process, even going to DC to interview with a Senator so I could get a congressional nomination."

"I realized kind of early on that it would be a tough road to go the civilian aviation route to the airlines. That's why I chose to enter the military because I thought it would be more of a guaranteed way to fly for a living." Dallas enjoyed the strong friendships he made at the Naval Academy. More importantly, his hard work soon paid off, graduating with distinction and being rewarded with a coveted pilot spot. Going into flight school, Dallas wanted to fly single-seat fighters. Again, he earned a spot, doing his initial tour in the F/A-18C Hornet. His next stop was the Navy Fighter Weapons School (TOPGUN) where after graduation he was asked to stay an additional three years as an instructor. A 20-year active-duty career in the Navy led to many more opportunities and experiences including multiple combat deployments and a tour as the Commanding Officer of a F/A-18E Super Hornet squadron.

## THE TRANSITION

"While serving as the Training Officer in a Super Hornet squadron stationed in Japan, I had my first opportunity to leave active-duty service if I wanted to. However, I realized that I didn't have all the pilot ratings I needed to get hired at an airline." Living overseas, Dallas knew how tough it would be to interview and get his stuff in order from the other side of the planet. "I basically decided that I might as well take the bonus (Aviation Department Head Retention Bonus) and stay in."

After his Department Head tour in a Hornet squadron, he was soon assigned to the Pentagon in Washington, DC and worked on the Joint Staff for the Chairman of the Joint Chief of Staff. While working in DC, Dallas met his wife. "I would say that it really started putting things more into perspective in terms of realizing there's a lot more to life than being in the military. It's all I had known since entering the Naval Academy." During his tour on the Joint Staff, Dallas was selected for command of Strike Fighter Squadron EIGHT ONE (VFA-81).

On his first deployment during his command tour, his wife was home expecting their first child. "And it was just a different feeling to be deployed, doing combat operations and having a wife at home and she's pregnant." Dallas made it home a couple weeks before his daughter was born. With his family growing, he knew it was time to retire.

"I made the decision going into my command tour I was going to retire and started talking to my friends who had already left active duty for the airlines." He considered a move to Charlotte to work for one of the major airlines. Says Dallas, "I had gotten my airline transport pilot rating (ATP) before I went to VFA-81." As he started researching what was required to start applying to the airlines, Dallas knew it would be quite different from his previous assignments. "I needed things like a civilian pilot rating, civilian medical qualification, and FCC radio license. I also had to have my driving record scrubbed and needed to write a resume. I even needed to take my military flight logbook and translate it into a civilian logbook."

Then the pandemic hit. "The airlines stopped hiring, so I shifted my attention to the cargo carriers, focusing my attention on FedEx." With a rigorous interview process, Dallas asked others working for the company (who were veterans from his previous squadrons) for some advice. "You had to do a knowledge test, which is really tough. I probably put in a month's worth of solid studying for it."

Dallas also needed a personal endorsement to get hired. "One of the guys I used to be in a squadron with who worked for me when I was a Department Head gave me his personal endorsement. I had another great friend who provided me with a ton of mentorship and help. He basically walked my resume to one of the chief pilots who also used to fly in the military. That was probably the difference in getting hired. They had roughly 30,000 applicants for about 1,000 spots so just getting your application looked at was an uphill battle." Dallas still flies for FedEx.

## LESSONS LEARNED

Excellence with humility. Perfection can be the goal, but we'll never achieve it. Learn from your mistakes and make sure others learn from your mistakes. Be thankful for the opportunities you've been blessed with and remain humble. Your successes are due to the efforts of many...life is a team sport.

## WHAT'S NEXT

Dallas' main focus right now is his family and sharing his love of aviation with others. "I'm so thankful that I was introduced to flying at a young age, and I want to give that same opportunity to other young men and women. Getting a job in the aviation world can be a very daunting task if you don't know where to start. I'm extremely grateful for the people in my life that helped steer me in the right direction. It's time to pay it forward."

## THE MILITARY EFFECT

"While on my second deployment in VFA-81, the COVID pandemic started. The aircraft carrier wasn't allowed to conduct any port calls due to COVID restrictions and communication with families back home was limited. Furthermore, we didn't know when we would be going home because the aircraft carriers that are coming to relieve us have to be COVID free. So, they have to sit off the coast for four weeks to make sure that no one has COVID." This was one of Dallas' more difficult leadership challenges. There was no end in sight to their deployment, which had already been extended by months. "I had sailors whose parents are passing away and they can't go home for funerals. I've got sailors who have orders that are coming up and they can't go back to execute their orders. Even worse, they don't know if they are going to lose their orders that they worked so hard to earn, and I don't have any good answers because I don't even know what's happening in the world back home...no one did." It was a tough time for everyone.

# 9

## DAN JARVIS, ARMY

linkedin.com/in/dan-jarvis-585708149
**Hometown:** *Winter Haven, Florida*
**Currently Resides:** *Winter Haven, Florida*

### WHY I SERVED

Coming from a family of veterans, Dan knew he wanted to continue the tradition. "At seventeen, my dad gave me two choices: pay rent or join the military. So, I went to see the Army recruiter without him. It was funny, because when the Army recruiter came to the house, my dad was so nice to the guy. Being from the Navy, I expected him to be mad, he took it better than I hoped. My mom, however, was an emotional wreck."

Not knowing what to expect, Dan did a two-year enlistment contract with the Army for the Army College Fund. "Four weeks later I was on a bus headed to Fort Benning, Georgia." After finishing his commitment, Dan went to college. Soon after, he got into law enforcement. Then 9/11 happened.

"I had a calling to go back in service because we were now in a state of war against global extremists. And if not me who, right?" Dan knew the military needed a lot of people. "I didn't even know if I was going to be able to get back in at that time, because I was 34 years old." He received a waiver and went back to basic training, doing it all over again. "With my experience and education, I got promoted quickly. My intention was to do a 20-year career. Dan's track was traditional. He deployed twice and was also Department of the Army, selected to be a drill sergeant.

### THE TRANSITION

On September 11 of 2014, Dan got medically discharged and had his retirement orders stamped. "There was pride that I went back in. To be able to deploy and fight alongside of some of America's finest warriors was very powerful. It was just ironic to finish my service on this date."

At the end of his deployment, Dan attended a Battalion Ball. "It's like the last Hooah! because orders start coming and people start changing duty stations. It's the last effort for the battalion to come together and celebrate as a unit." At this celebration many Wounded Warriors were in attendance. "One of the gentlemen that came was Don Eslinger, Sr., father of Donny Eslinger, my wounded warrior. He was the elected sheriff of Seminole County, Florida. He talked to me into going back into law enforcement." This lasted for two years.

In his early 40's, the physical tolls of Dan's career caught up. "When that uniform came off, is when everything for me kind of unraveled. It was a tough period, and I was sick and tired of being sick and tired, and I decided I got to find a better way because I wanted help. When I started looking for other alternatives to heal myself, I stumbled onto some things that were pretty profound. It was a massive paradigm shift. I realized, wow, why is this not available to everybody?"

While working at the Sheriff's office, Dan met a retired Army Lieutenant Colonel. "He invited me to come to a men's leadership retreat in Tampa, where I met some pretty cool people." The event was attended by nearly forty vets, first responders, and civilians. "One of the gentlemen, an Air Force vet, was involved with an organization doing an alternative treatment for PTSD. During his presentation he stopped and looked at me. It was a pivotal point in life. He says, 'Dan, you look like you have something you want to say.' And I said, 22 Zero, just like that." The presenter was confused and asked for clarification. "We're losing twenty-two vets a day to suicide, and we are going to take it to zero."

And so, the idea was launched. "I had no idea how we were going to do it." Dan immediately started the process to incorporate 22Zero in the state of Florida. It was April 18, 2018.

## LESSONS LEARNED

Model the success of the people around you and then start adapting your own communication styles.

## WHAT'S NEXT

22Zero (www.22zero.org) was formed in 2018 as a 501c3. "We're trying to find a way to stand in the gap and help provide resources to vets and first responders." Even with funding tough since COVID, the group moves on, developing the Trauma Resiliency Protocol for trauma and PTSD, and the Emotions Management Process for emotions like anxiety and anger. "So, I learned as much as I could in developing our processes and we started doing our own research."

"Since the pandemic, everything has changed. The veil was lifted from the mental health world." Dan knows that more people need to get treated. "When the tele-health world took off, it was a game changer. 22Zero now has coaches all over the country. "Now when people come to us needing help, they've already acknowledged they've got a problem. All we do is evaluate them like a triage and assign them a coach." Dan is often asked the difference between in-person and tele-health. "The difference is zero. The results are identical."

Dan recently launched Tactical Resiliency, LLC, a training company (https://tacticalresiliencytraining.com), teaching the 22Zero protocols to active military, first responders and mental health professionals. "It was created to spread healing beyond our nonprofit 22Zero into the world. 22Zero is streamlined to a state of effective execution and now we are bridging others with skills to tackle and conquer life with the highest level of human potential." Tactical Resiliency, LLC wants to fund 22Zero to expand their reach. "We train active police departments. We train fire departments. We train members of the US border patrol to be able to do peer to peer. The key is 22Zero can't handle one million vets."

## THE MILITARY EFFECT

"Get plugged back into your local community of veterans, whether it's an American Legion or a VFW. Find some kind of organization that you can be a part of because you've got to restructure the tribe. You can't sit out there. Isolation is the biggest killer."

# 10

## DIANA VILLA, ARMY

**Hometown:** *Houston, Texas*
**Currently Resides:** *Bradenton, Florida*

## WHY I SERVED

Diana was born in Houston, Texas but her parents moved to Colombia, South America when she was four. After her parents divorced, her mother, in search of a better future for her two daughters, returned to the U.S when Diana was 15. Diana did not know English and felt out of place. Her childhood dream was to become a doctor, so she diligently worked hard to graduate early, and she did so at the age of 17.

With only two years of being in the United States, and not being familiar with the education system, in addition to not having the financial means, Diana's high school counselor told her, "Someone like you, will never graduate high school, yet alone go to college." As Diana saw her dream of being a doctor fade away, something sparked the idea that she needed to pursue other options and that nothing was going to stop her from achieving her dream.

In high school, Diana met her high school sweetheart, "He was the first Colombian I met, and I could speak Spanish with him. I felt an immediate connection." After dating for two years and with graduation quickly approaching, it was time to decide their future. "His cousin had joined the army, so my boyfriend (at the time) joined too". She was told that the army was paying for his education. " I knew this was the opportunity I needed. Not once did I think about the sacrifice, I only thought of the result." With her mother's permission, Diana joined at 17 and was assigned to become a medical specialist (91 Bravo). "I saw this as the greatest opportunity for me to reach my goals and be the first one on my mother's side of the family to go to college." Everyone told her she could not do it, and her high school counselor finished up with the discouraging words, 'That's the best thing for someone like you.'"

Basic training was a challenge, and her five-foot two-inch, 115 lbs. frame did not make things easier. During basic training, Diana's boyfriend and she communicated only by letters. In one of those he proposed. Diana stated, "On Sundays I used the public phone booth to call his mom, using a calling card. It was another way to find out how he was doing."

As Diana was finishing her medical training, she received assignment orders to be stationed in Germany and her boyfriend received orders to go to California. The two got married one weekend, as her boyfriend was en route to his first duty station. The marriage kept them together, instead of going to separate bases in different countries and after 26 years they are still going strong. "What prompted me to join the Army was my desire to accomplish my dream and be a doctor. I needed the money for college, but once in, the camaraderie, the leadership and the service to my country became the driving force." The Army changed her life. She discovered a new sense of empowerment and resilience she had never experienced. She moved quickly through the ranks and became a Sergeant at the age of 20.

## THE TRANSITION

In 2001, Diana's husband reclassified and was sent to Fort Campbell, Kentucky on an unaccompanied tour. "We were apart for six months, and my re-enlistment was coming up. I was going to be sent to Korea". Valuing her relationship more, Diana made the decision to leave the military in August of 2001, "It was a very difficult decision because I loved what I did, but my marriage came first."

Diana wasn't ready to close the military chapter of her life, so she went to the National Guard on September 10th, 2001, to serve again. She was asked to come back the next morning, but Diana couldn't as she was flying to Texas, "The next morning I woke up to the detrimental sight of the twin towers collapsing and I swore they were going to activate me".

With her husband at Air Assault school and in lockdown, Diana went back to Fort Hood to visit the unit she had just finished with. She told her commander, "I want to volunteer, please put me back in. They told me it doesn't work that way. You must wait until they call you." With both trying to get back home, her husband's unit got activated. Even with both wanting to go and defend their country, her husband was assigned to recruiting duty.

Shortly after Diana and her husband relocated to Chicago, she enrolled at the University of Illinois, "I eventually wanted to have children and didn't want us to be dual military with kids". She went to work for the Navy in a before/after school care program, enjoying the work so much that Diana switched her major to education.

Now a military spouse, Diana still had a desire to serve. She served as an FRG (Family Readiness Group leader) supporting her husband in his military career while giving up hers. As a military spouse, the family moved from base to base every two years. Being a teacher, Diana had to re-certify in every state, "By the time you finish unpacking and get used to a new routine, it's time to leave again. It was tough on the kids, tough being a single married mom, tough to have continuity in a career, and tough to build relationships." But Diana pressed on, once getting great advice, " You grow where you are planted, so that's what we did."

In 2017 her husband was medically discharged after battling health issues and in 2018 they moved to Florida. Diana became his full-time caregiver along with caring for and homeschooling her three boys. It was a challenging time, and she leaned heavily on her faith. Seeing her husband go from a GI Joe to someone who needed her 100% was a difficult journey, "My only support was my small Bible study group from the chapel's office and the community of other military spouses."

After leaving the military, her network expanded, and she was able to attend a retreat. It was a life changing trip, "I was so stressed and had no relief. I was drowning and had no support; I stopped dreaming and found my life meaningless."

During a retreat, a social worker met with Diana and asked her, "What did you enjoy doing before all this happened?" That question became the catalyst for change and gave Diana the energy to start investing in herself once again. She loved CrossFit but couldn't afford it at the time, "When I told him I did CrossFit, the organization gifted me a six-month membership, working out was the only time I had to myself and the only time my problems were on pause. I met all these other spouses that were in the same place that I was. It became our new community." She goes on to say, " There's a different world out here. Leaving the military is hard. It was the only life we had known since we were 17, and after twenty years of service we got out and lost our identity. We're not active duty anymore, and we're not civilians, so where do we belong? We started being each other's resources and support."

## LESSONS LEARNED

NO! means find another way. Don't allow your circumstances to determine your future.

## WHAT'S NEXT

After she began investing in herself, in 2020, Diana continued her education, "I wanted to do something to give back." She desired to work or find a military nonprofit organization that helped veterans and military spouses. She got her master's degree in organizational leadership with a concentration in coaching and mentoring. In 2021, she was given the opportunity to volunteer as a peer leader and mentor with the Wounded Warrior Project supporting a program for military spouses. She jumped right in, "As a peer leader, I get to encourage and help those spouses that were where I was five years ago. I also obtained my Life Coach certification and started my Life Coaching and Consulting business. My passion is to give back to our veterans and families. I don't ever want a veteran or spouse to feel like they are alone and have no support."

# THE MILITARY EFFECT

"As a military spouse, it never matters how full your hands are, we will give whatever is needed. As a veteran, we will always be serving as we leave no one behind."

# D.J. VANAS, AIR FORCE

linkedin.com/in/djvanas
**Hometown:** *Muskegon, Michigan*
**Currently Resides:** *San Diego, California*

## WHY I SERVED

DJ was born while his dad was in basic training. "He enlisted in the Air Force, and I grew up as an Air Force brat at the end of a runway. We lived in enlisted housing my whole life." For DJ, it was fascinating to watch his dad come home from work every day. "He worked for strategic air command and was on an air crew for several years. When he would come home, I'd see him in his uniform and boots."

Those years on the base left an impression on DJ. "I knew he was doing important work that had meaning. I remember his patch. It had an iron gauntlet with lightning coming out of it and was super cool."

"I was always fascinated with aviation space back to my earliest memories and wanted to be a pilot. My parents ruined me with my first flight lesson for my 13th birthday. They didn't know what they were starting with that." DJ begged for over a month till they relented. "They said, fine, if you want do this, you can, but you need to keep all your grades up, A's and B's only. You have to stay out of trouble. You have to make your own money for lessons."

DJ flew all through high school for the civil air patrol. "By the time I got to the Air Force Academy, I had 365 hours logged in three different types of aircraft." Participating in Junior ROTC also, he was headed on the path towards the military. "My number one pick was the Air Force Academy, and I was accepted". During his second week of basic training, DJ was informed that he failed his physical and would never fly, even as a navigator. "I knew my eyes weren't great, because I had contacts all through high school." The news was devastating.

With no back up plan, DJ took a quick assessment of his life. Realizing he was at an incredible institution and making great friends, and with a shaved head, he decided to wait till it grew out. "Four years later, I'm throwing up my hat and the Thunderbirds are screaming over." He soon went into the officer ranks of the Air Force. "I stayed back for a year, at the Air Force Academy, helping them to increase diversity and recruiting. I basically went up and kind of complained that we had this great institution, but only a handful of us were native or tribal members."

DJ's career path took him into systems acquisition working in space warfare. We built and launched satellites as part of our space components for the Air Force." While stationed out in LA, he got his master's degree at the University of Southern Cal. Soon, DJ became the Chief of Minority Enrollment (now called the Office of Diversity) at the Air Force Academy, holding that position for four years.

## THE TRANSITION

Slated to get out in October of 2001, a "stop loss' went into effect as the result of 9/11. "The problem with that is I had geared up my schedule and had speaking commitments that I made." It was terrifying for DJ. "I was speaking for free on the side. Whenever I was at native education conferences for tribal communities. people would call and say: "Can you come to our education conference and work with our tribal youth?" He was forced to burn up all his leave time. "I felt like I had two full-time jobs, especially towards the last couple months of that that time period. It was extremely stressful."

"In 2002, I left as a captain and halfway through a military career. Everybody thought I was nuts to leave at that point. Ready to be a speaker, I found what I wanted to do more than anything, which was get out and do this on my own. I never looked back." Says DJ, "I had a lot of good mentors in the National Speaker Association that were really encouraging and kind of helped me build things."

In his first year, DJ went from small groups to big groups and really got well versed. He was ready to begin to present publicly. "I remember well, the first time I got paid to speak. I was at USC getting my master's and it was Native American Heritage Month." He was asked to come and speak on contemporary native issues in our society. Says DJ, "I showed up and did the program and they hand me a check for one hundred dollars. They said, 'here's your honorarium.' I'm like, what is that? I remembered looking at it, and I walked out." It was the first time he had an inkling that this might lead to something else.

## LESSONS LEARNED

Honor what you've been through and who you are, by using your talent, ability and skill to serve others.

## WHAT'S NEXT

The majority of D.J.'s focus now is with Native organizations. "There's all kinds of national native organizations, like in healthcare and education through Head Start. I work at all different levels in our tribal communities. I am always trying to create better leaders, and more effective employees."

He also continues to engage with Fortune 500 companies like AllState & Applied Materials. "Every one of those big companies has a native employee resource group. I'll continue to seek more international opportunities for the community and myself."

"I think I've been an entrepreneur all my life. Even when I was a little kid, I'd make crafts to sell so I had money for Christmas presents". DJ loves talking about his cultural background. "That's always been a big part of my life." He's now working hard promoting his third book, *The Warrior Within.* "I'm enjoying where I am in my career. I feel like I've hit my stride. I've not taken my foot off the gas in any sense of that word."

## THE MILITARY EFFECT

"Do not sell yourself short on all the things that you have gathered during your time in uniform. We tend to downplay that to a degree that I think is shocking. We take it for granted in a really serious way. That doesn't help us. We need to be able to look back and be inspired by what we've done, what we've created, what we've learned, and the experiences that we have. There is a plethora of stuff coming out of the military that we learned that we could bring to bear, and that we can contribute to any organization that we join."

# 12

## GARTH MASSEY, MARINES

linkedin.com/in/garthmassey
**Hometown:** *Anchorage, Alaska*
**Currently Resides:** *Greenville, South Carolina*

## WHY I SERVED

Born and raised in Alaska, Garth grew up the son of an architect. His dad was a hippie with hair hanging down to his belt, graduating from Cal Berkely in the 60's, moving to Alaska to avoid the draft. While in and out of college, Garth traveled the country by motorcycle, eventually running out of gas in San Diego, where he decided to stop and finish his degree. "I got on a few athletic teams and became a beach lifeguard." He met a girl whose father was in the Navy Reserves and thought that might be a great side gig, only to learn they don't let you join as a Navy Captain.

It was the exact opposite of what his dad had done, but Garth moved forward practically on a dare. "I thought the Navy looked pretty cool. I was a junior getting ready to graduate but walked straight to the ROTC office." He was told that the minimum requirement was two more years of school studying military science. Not wanting to extend his college any more than he had to, he visited the Army and Air Force. They gave the same answer. And then came the Marine Corps "They said all I needed was a college degree. Then they told me I probably wouldn't be able to finish the application process, as it normally takes most candidates a month. I was back in three days." He was soon accepted and began the journey.

## THE TRANSITION

"It was a quiet time. There were no wars and we just trained, so I got out". Having a brand-new baby, Garth and his wife started considering their lifestyle. Says Garth, "The economy was strong, and they were throwing jobs at people. I went to 12 interviews and got 8 job offers". The alternative was more deployment and time in the field. With a new baby and plans for more Garth took the new job offer.

They moved to Orange County, California and Garth immediately looked into the Reserves. "One of the senior enlisted Marines I had served with heard I was getting out and gave me a call. He said, 'You have to join this unit. So, I did. That unit ended up being the first reserve infantry battalion activate after 9/11". The following January he was on orders and training at Camp Pendleton and then extended a second year to join the opening invasion in Iraq.

For two years Garth held a traditional job. "I traveled all week for work then packed a different bag and flew somewhere for drill." The travel between the two lives got to be a lot, as the pressure at home mounted not to be gone one weekend a month and two weeks in the summer. Says Garth, "Do the math. Weigh the pros and cons. It makes no sense. It's really an irrational call to service". The math does not tell the whole story. "To tell the whole story you have to pay attention to the type of person you want to be. Does service, honor and self-development play into the equation? I missed time at home,but I defined myself as a Marine, it was core to my identity, you can't walk away from yourself,so you keep giving."

"At my last job, I realized the sales team was not planning for the meetings". Garth used one of the models from the Marines planning tool kit to teach his sales team how to prepare. "It is the five-paragraph order just translated into five steps for a sales call." The president of the company, who was also a former Marine, recognized this immediately. "He asked me to train the same thing to the entire company". Things kept growing and after 3 ½ years treating teaching like a hobby, Garth realized it could be a career. "So, I quit and started my own company."

When Garth launched his company, called CommandReady, everyone who hired him was a veteran. "I might not have served with them, but they recognized the pitch and wanted to hire me. I would tell veterans my company teaches squad leader school, preparing sergeants to lead small teams, and they all got it. You could do a lot if you had a couple good sergeants in your company." He goes on to say, "Someone in the organization was a vet, and they wanted to get the level of training the military gives, but with applications in their current business".

Now Garth teaches the elements of planning, decision making, and leadership across the country. "It's allowed me to continue in the Reserves. I set my speaking calendar and workshops; the rest is online learning. Both lives fit in a very complimentary way". He has commanded infantry units up to command of a regiment and is currently the officer in charge of a training program at the Training and Education Command. Garth left active duty in 2001 and has nearly 4 1/2 years of mobilization with the Reserves, as he goes into his 29th year of service.

## LESSONS LEARNED

Reflect before you react.

## WHAT'S NEXT

"We want to reach more organizations looking to grow people". Carefully growing his network, Garth is going back to basics. "I'm Constantly working through my phone to see who I haven't spoken to in a while." He's also busy publishing his first book, *The Beginning of Quitting*. "It talks about how our leadership directly affects the people we work with and our ability to recruit and retain talent."

One day Garth hopes to open a leadership retreat center. "I would love to have a place where people would go to get experiential hands-on opportunities to test themselves physically and mentally, but also to find a place of solitude and be still...so they can learn to reflect before they react.

## THE MILITARY EFFECT

When you find the networks of veteran business owners, it is very connected and supportive. Says Garth, " We are a service-based culture, and value people who give. But then you come out to the civilian world, it's a pride-based culture. LinkedIn put out some stats a while ago that said military veterans are the most connected group on their platform".

# 13

## GENE MORAN, NAVY

linkedin.com/in/genemoran
**Hometown:** *Boca Raton, Florida*
**Currently Resides:** *Bradenton, Florida*

## WHY I SERVED

"As a teenager I recognized that important people in my life had attributed their success to their time in the Navy. My father's uncle who had served in World War II and rose to be the chairman of John Hancock Insurance made an imprint". Another close family friend in South Florida was a Navy reservist who Gene sailed offshore sailboats with. "I knew I wanted to get some of that experience."

Gene saw the Navy as a logical path, thinking he would spend four or five years there. His career ended up going more than 24 years. Time on the water seemed familiar to him. Getting in his first ship, Gene understood relative motion in ways that most people at that point in their career didn't fully appreciate. "I was a pretty proficient ship handler early on, and I just naturally adapted to it."

"In the military, success builds upon success. If you demonstrate initiative and basic talent, people will invest in you, train you, and position you for bigger and better things." Gene says, "I was told before I took my first ship command that there will probably be only two or three times when I absolutely have to make an incredibly snap decision. It has to be right. It just can't be wrong. That guidance and recognition of perspective happened to me over and over again in the Navy."

"I can distinctly remember at the nine-year mark; I believe I can be a Captain in the Navy of my own ship." Through some great support and opportunities, Gene moved up the ranks quickly. "I was in command of my first ship at the 15-year mark. That was quite early. Here I was at age 38 in command of a destroyer, and then four years later commanding a cruiser."

"Deciding to continue in a very senior role is a family decision," says Gene. "There is so much time away, and you need that support. It's a level of commitment not seen in many corporate roles. There are people that do what we call geographic bachelor tours, where the work might be in one place and the family stays somewhere else". He continues, "that wasn't for us, and we recognized when it was time to transition."

# THE TRANSITION

"As one progresses in a career, you begin to recognize there are logical building blocks, like increasing education and responsibility. During my time, society was going through a transition of its own with true dual income families," says Gene.

The system was signaling there was a future for Gene, but he wasn't thinking that way. "I came to recognize that I was more interested in trying my hand in business and understanding corporate life, and maybe having some different experiences." At home, his four daughters were in critical years. "They were either coming of age for college, entering it, or on the cusp of leaving."

At the 24-year mark, Gene felt it was time to leave. "I was on vacation with the family and mapping out on an index card what life would look like financially if I stayed in or got out. It became a very easy decision." He still has that index card.

"Being a political science major at Florida State, there was a natural interest to work in the government sector." Even while on sea duty, Gene always knew he wanted to go to Washington. "I didn't know exactly what that meant, but there was some draw, a calling to work at that level and be a part of it." He goes on to say, "When I got into a couple of Washington jobs, I recognized that there was a Navy program where and this happens across government you can be a congressional fellow for one year. So, while on active duty as a senior commander, post destroyer command, I worked in the office of former Senator Thad Cochran, who at the time was a senior defense appropriator." This experience gave Gene the insight into how differently Congress is organized and how they think in general about problem solving.

"I was a little unique in that in my senior shore assignments, I was representing the Navy to Congress in a couple of different roles. So, I was in a position to be an advisor to the Secretary of the Navy and Chief of Naval Operations about things that were happening in Congress and coordinating with committees on things that dealt with broader Navy and national security policy." Gene was able to travel with members of Congress, including notables like Senators John McCain, Lindsey Graham, and Joe Lieberman. Gene says, " I did international travel with them and got really tremendous exposure to different kinds of interactions that naturally take place between the services, industry and government." His experiences made Gene very attractive to defense companies in Washington. "For me, the barrier to leaving the active duty was fairly easy."

While leaving was easy, the transition proved to be more difficult. "Even with many opportunities it took a few years for me to recognize that I really was not fulfilled in the corporate world." After a few years, Gene made the jump to become an independent consultant and lobbyist where he could have that sense of control and the ability to invest in himself the way he had on active duty. "It wasn't until I left the military that I appreciated how geographically diverse my network was."

## LESSONS LEARNED

Don't be afraid to try something different.

## WHAT'S NEXT

"We should always be looking for ways to be more efficient and remove man-made friction points between how we do things. I embrace it." Gene's entire business is in the cloud. He was one of the millions who was part of the data breach at the Office of Personal Management with the US Government. "I think the expectation of privacy has changed dramatically and we need to get on with it and recognize that there are protocols that can be put in place to protect things as much as possible."

Gene recently completed his PhD in Public Policy. "This ability to continue to evolve has been a major learning point at this stage of life. I see too many people not doing that." His 5th book, *Government Deals are Funded, Not Sold,* published in late 2023. Much of Gene's business comes from digital networking. "Being present in this way allows me to be accessible for new opportunities and making introductions for others."

A boater all his life, Gene has come to understand the yachting world better recognizing similarities with ship systems. "There are a lot of crossover systems and commonality that are not the shiny white parts of the boat, but the mechanical and electrical architectures. Some of my primary defense clients are suppliers working in both industries." To him, it made perfect sense to attend these boat shows and make connections. "I was quickly connected with the US Super Yacht Association, and the Shipbuilders Council of America, where there was some crossover. " It's a classic networking story, but the only way it came about was because I tried something different and put myself in a position to meet different people."

"I believe in this country, really, around the world, anybody can do this sort of thing with a little bit of effort. Mostly, they are afraid, they don't have enough imagination, or they don't let their imagination take them to a place where they might consider, hey, could I do something over here? And maybe that's part of being somewhat entrepreneurial. I wouldn't describe myself as a swashbuckling entrepreneur, but I do take some risks and I try different things, and I think I'm measured and calculated about it."

## THE MILITARY EFFECT

When you are dealing with veterans, it would be extremely rare to question whether a veteran told you the truth. Says Gene, "I think there's a misperception by those that have not served that it's all about barking orders and control by authority. Authority is a part of how any complex organization works. But you have to have buy-in from the people around you about what the mission is and why it's important. That takes extra forms of communication, and there's a lot of different ways to do that in all the services. We really spend a lot of time growing leaders to help teach these sorts of concepts."

## 14

# GEORGE KOVATCH, COAST GUARD

linkedin.com/in/george-e-kovatch-73a08a3
**Hometown:** *Hingham, Massachusetts*
**Currently Resides:** *Virginia*

## WHY I SERVED

Seeking one last fun summer job while in college, George had no idea how this decision would change his life forever. Growing up fishing off Cape Cod, his first choice was to work as a deckhand on a sportfishing boat. But those jobs were hard to come by. While in Woods Hole, Massachusetts he noticed the Coast Guard Station. This would begin his new adventure.

It was 1990, pre-9/11, and back then you could still walk into an office for the Coast Guard. "They thought I wanted to enlist, but all I wanted was a summer job. I think they just wanted to get rid of me and said I should go to the district headquarters in Boston. So, I did." It was a Friday and George was told to come back on Monday to be interviewed for a summer internship. That Monday he was hired.

"I didn't know much about the Coast Guard, other than they were out on the water. I spent that whole summer working for a chief warrant officer boatswain's mate in the administration office and wasn't outside on the boats, but it taught me a lot about the Coast Guard." At the end of the summer his boss asked George if he wanted to make some extra money working through his senior year of college. He jumped at the opportunity though it was not easy getting up at 5am on Tuesdays & Thursdays (that's tough in college) taking the "T" to work.

Graduating in 1991 as a business major was not good timing. It was a recession year. George was offered a job on the stock exchange as a floor runner making commission only. With no way to get to New York and no money for an apartment, he had no chance of getting this job. At the same time, the Coast Guard made an offer to start as a GS-3 (basically entry level) making $17,000/year. He took it!

"I absolutely loved it. Everyone treated me so well because I was in kind of an unusual space. I was not active duty, and I was a brand-new civilian, so they tried to recruit me to go to Officer Candidate School right from day one. I worked directly for a Captain who was the Chief of Administration. He was very supportive of my career."

Every few weeks his boss would tell him that the next day he would not be in the office. Instead, George got sent to the nearby small boat station, he flew in helicopters and jets, and he worked closely with the rescue teams. Then the Halloween Storm (later made famous by the Book/Movie *The Perfect Storm* occurred in October of 1991. As the District Awards Board clerk, all the awards for this famous rescue came across George's desk, "It was the most amazing rescue story I had ever read about. I said to myself, this is what I want to do! I went to Officer Candidate School in 1993. My goal was to be the captain of a ship." Being an Officer Candidate School Graduate was more challenging in the early 1990s than it is now. You did not always compete for the best opportunities. George knew the best way to control his career path was through back-to-back sea assignments to become a patrol boat captain, so he took some tough assignments and finally got his first patrol boat command in Miami.

At last, George was accepted to Columbia Business School. "After this I was assigned to Coast Guard Headquarters in Washington, DC. Nobody joins the Coast Guard to get a desk job at Headquarters, but I learned to make the most of it and was rewarded by meeting so many people and learning about the business side of the service in the CFO's office." After helping the Coast Guard achieve its first CFO audit compliance in its history, George went back to sea as a Commander. He was then selected to serve on the Senate Appropriations Committee as a Coast Guard fellow. "The Coast Guard does a fantastic job of strategically placing folks on Capitol Hill." At this point he could write his own ticket to any job he wanted. "It was a two-year assignment. I guess they liked me enough that they asked if I would stay a third year, so I did." His decision to stay a third year brought him over the 20 years of service mark. His position led to enough attractive job offers that, combined with the long-term needs of a young family, led to his decision to transition from Active Duty.

## THE TRANSITION

"My colleague on the Appropriations Committee, a retired Marine, and I were talking about whether I should retire from the military. He offered to set up some "informational" lunch meetings." One of those lunches was with Gene Moran (USN retired, also in the book) he was at the time working for DRS, a large defense company. "He and I just hit it off right away. At the end of the lunch, he said, "George, I know this was just an informational meeting, but I think our company would be wise to hire you."

"It is a decision we all eventually face, and I had to give it some thought. Timing was important, and I was told that the opportunity may not exist if I went back to another ship for two more years. The other factor was my wife and I got married later in life, we didn't have kids until I was 40 years old. So, when I was at the 20-year mark, my daughter was three and my son one." George could have stayed another 10 years in the Coast Guard. "But then I would still have relatively young children so I would have to find a second career at that point. Plus, we probably would have moved four or five more times."

It wasn't until he took a "love-view" look at his career (instead of just looking the typical two years out at the next command opportunity), that the decision became clear. George loved the Coast Guard and wanted to go back to a ship just one more time; his wife reminded him "Even your admiral friends said they'd like to go back one more time, so no matter how many times you go back there will always be that desire for 'one more time'."

After retiring from the Coast Guard, George spent a few years with a mid-sized defense consulting company. Then he was asked to return to government as a Senior Executive Service member at the Department of Homeland Security. Four years later, he was asked by the Under Secretary of the Navy to come to the Pentagon and lead their Chief Management Office. For his last government position, he was asked to serve as the Deputy Comptroller for the Department of Defense (a job he was nominated for by his same former Senate Appropriations Committee colleague).

As DoD Deputy Comptroller he had six senior military leaders working for him. It was impossible to keep tabs on everything happening across the DoD, but George never worried. "With six Colonels/Captains, most of whom had come from a major command, I knew they had great judgment, were trustworthy, and loyal to the mission. So, I would tell them, 'These are the three things the Secretary of Defense really cares about. If any of these things hit your radar, I want to know about it. Other than that, you take care of things and let me know of anything you think might soon become a problem. I think there is something that's ingrained in the military culture that instills trust." George also witnessed several senior leaders throughout Washington who didn't take advantage of that military culture.

"At least a year before you retire, start doing some exploratory networking. If you wait until you retire, it is definitely much more difficult." George was fortunate. "I had no plans to retire from the Coast Guard, but when I got extended for that extra year, it offered me the opportunity to get out there and meet people in other industries and companies." He remembers being tired of yet another lunch meeting, but realized, "You learn something from everybody you meet, and you never know where or when you will pick up that valuable nugget of information or connection. So, I would take the meeting, get a sense of what's out there and just be open to listening."

George shared another transition story with me. "I knew a retiring Marine Colonel in the Special Forces who flew H-60 combat search and rescue missions. He did four tours in Iraq. From Alabama, the veteran had spent seven years away from his family and was ready to go home. He said, I don't know what I'm going to do when I retire. I guess I'm just going to become a contractor and do the same combat search and rescue as a contractor and go back to Iraq. The only thing I know how to do is move people and equipment in and out of hostile locations on short notice. I was like, you know what? You need to investigate FEMA in the Department of Homeland Security. Because they move people and equipment in and out of places in response to natural disasters." George knew it would be a job close to home and tried to get the Marine to think about new possibilities. "He didn't know anything about FEMA or DHS because his network was so tightly revolved around his current world. To this day, I'd love to find out where he ended up."

## LESSONS LEARNED

Career progression is so important on a resume in any industry. Always be trending up.

## WHAT'S NEXT

Since leaving the Pentagon, George started his own Consulting and Government Relations company KSA Federal. He serves as a trusted advisor to companies and government agencies to help them improve their business with the Departments of Defense and Homeland Security and navigate the complexities of the Federal Budgeting Process. He also helps small to mid-sized innovative companies raise funding and bring their new ideas to the Department of Defense. He is a frequent speaker at America Society of Military Comptrollers (ASMC) events and has supported efforts to improve the Department of Defense's Planning, Programming, Budgeting, and Execution (PPBE) process.

George is also proud to have been recently appointed to the Board of Directors for the U.S. Naval Sea Cadets Corps. This organization is the Navy's Youth Development Program. The Board's goal is to greatly increase participation in Sea Cadets. "Most of those who join the military do so because they come from military families. We need to improve our efforts to recruit more broadly, or we will run out of volunteers. The Sea Cadet program should be as well-known and as large as the Boy & Girl Scouts. Service teaches great life lessons. We are excited to share these opportunities with the next generation."

Public service clearly is instilled in George's sense of patriotism. "There really is no more noble calling than to serve one's country. I hope to continue to do so in one capacity or another."

George continues to receive encouragement in writing a book. "If I can figure out how to organize all these different life lessons and career advice. I love being a mentor and strongly relate to the definition of a mentor being 'someone whose hindsight can become someone else's foresight. I have had some good mentors throughout my career, and I enjoy returning the favor."

# THE MILITARY EFFECT

"I've found that people value either your expertise or your network (or your money, but that is a separate issue). Both of those things you must work on to improve and keep refreshing. I think that people in the military have a leg up on non-military because of the culture, the leadership and the trust instilled in us all. Where we sometimes need to push ourselves is expanding our network so we can articulate how our military expertise translates into the civilian world. When I was deciding whether to retire or not, it was eye opening for me to realize that people I looked to as mentors when I was coming up the ranks, were now asking me for advice and introductions. That's when I realized I had built a solid network."

# 15

## HEATHER THRONE, ARMY

linkedin.com/in/heather-throne-westpoint
**Hometown:** *Jupiter, Florida*
**Currently Resides:** *Woodstock, Georgia*

## WHY I SERVED

Growing up in a blue-collar family, Heather's parents were determined to get her to college. Touring West Point with her father she knew immediately, "I belong here."

It was an experience she will never forget. "It didn't take long to understand why serving made sense for me." Drawn to the idea of service, being in the military resonated with Heather. The motto, the mission, and taking the financial burden off her parents were huge factors. While there she thought, "Wow, wouldn't it be cool to go into aviation?"

Up until the early 90's, women could go into a certain number of branches, but were limited to those classified as 'combat' branches. Unlike today, infantry, armor and field artillery are all fully open. "President Bush opened up combat aviation to women in the 90's and I wanted that mission," said Heather. With a strong desire to enter the Aviation branch, she was determined to get into the attack branch of aviation.

Heather naturally acclimated to the routine, the regiment, the discipline that comes along with the military. She also enjoyed the softer feeling of patriotism and service. "I knew coming out of West Point that likely we were going to go somewhere in the world and serve. That becomes something people want to do."

She spent a year at Fort Rucker in Alabama, attending the initial rotary wing course, followed by the AH-64-A Apache helicopter transition course. Heather went on to be assigned to the 1/-229th Attack Helicopter Battalion at Fort Bragg, NC as the first woman aviator and second lieutenant in that battalion. Says Heather, "I was very fortunate that there were really fantastic pilots, and leaders who were proponents of me, as a woman, being there. I worked hard to be the best aviator and lieutenant I could ever be."

# THE TRANSITION

"Early on, when I was young, single, not married, and without kids, I thought I could do this forever. It's a fast pace, you are in the field or deployed, and working lots of hours." Heather soon got married to another helicopter pilot and had her first child. " It no longer matched up to what we wanted for our family. We didn't want to both be gone and have our child cared for by the family network. Being good parents and raising our family became our number one mission."

Not wanting to place the burden on anyone else, they both made the decision to transfer out. "It was all we had known our entire adult life, wearing that uniform. It took a lot of effort to figure out who's going to hire us and for what role."

"My first job was with a company founded by two Air Force Academy grads. They knew what they wanted, and they hired a lot of young service academy leaders." From there, Heather went on to Siemens. "My resume didn't translate well to the job role, but they took a gamble on me. I think it paid off because I've worked with them almost 18 years total."

# LESSONS LEARNED

"I take the values, the lessons, and the people who I connected with to heart today, because I think those relationships are the fundamental basis for who I am as a grown up. I often reflect on these topics to guide me today."

# WHAT'S NEXT

Heather is a fan of LinkedIn, building it intentionally from a business perspective. "I will add most anyone to my network. But the true people that I think are my network are those that aren't going to call me just when they need something from me. Whenever I do connect, I write down their name, who they are, and then commonality, things that I'll remember. I make it a personal mission to connect others."

She knows with social media we have to let some of it in, but also be guarded. "I don't like some of the elements. Sometimes we as parents have allowed social media and electronics to fill that void where you didn't feel like parenting. Social media and electronics cannot replace human interaction and finding that balance is important."

"People have lost the knack of walking into a room and shaking hands. I often wonder if it's because of the Pandemic, social media or just a new habit created by adults."

Exercise is important in Heather's life, and she spends some time coaching CrossFit to others in a community where everyone is an athlete. "I have five F's: Family, Friends, Freedom, Fitness and Fun. These underscore the significance of a holistic approach to well-being."

Focus on family is a central theme in Heather's life. Two of her sons are planning to serve in the United States Coast Guard upon graduation from the USGA. Heather believes a strong family bond and supportive environment has promoted all four children to explore their interests and aspirations (she has another son on the way to college, and an active daughter in middle school).

Heather looks forward to the not so far off future and officially becoming an empty nester, traveling, and seeing the world with her husband of over 25 years.

## THE MILITARY EFFECT

'You want to talk about the difference of decision-making over the ocean, going 100 knots with no ambient light, or worrying about a document getting out. I don't sweat the small stuff at corporate America because I've sweated in much tougher circumstances while flying a helicopter."

# 16

## J SCOT HEATHMAN, AIR FORCE

linkedin.com/in/jscotheathman
**Hometown:** *Rochester, Minnesota*
**Currently Resides:** *Shiloh, Illinois*

## WHY I SERVED

Scot was born to serve from the day he was born at Offutt Air Force Base in Nebraska. His mother was a nurse, and his father was an Air Force Airman. "My dad was drafted right out of high school in 1969, so he decided to enlist in the Air Force." Following his father's 4-year tour, and the birth of Scot, his family moved to South Dakota. And that's when something special happened. "I remember seeing Star Wars when it first came out and being blown away by the Millennium Falcon. That's what I want to do! I want to fly!" Later in life, Scot found himself flying tankers and cargo planes in the Air Force, supporting Air Mobility Command and the organization formally known as SAC. "I feel very blessed to have chased and captured my dream."

Living a life of service was important to Scot's family, whether it was through 4-H, the church or just in the local community, but he envisioned something much bigger than himself. "I knew I had gone to college in order to become an officer and possibly fly in the Air Force, but for me, it was really about serving my country which drew me to a career of military service." He competed and earned a 3-year scholarship through the Air Force Reserve Officer Training Corps (AFROTC) and attended Illinois Tech in Chicago. I was blessed, as the Air Force funded quite bit of my civil engineering degree while the school supplemented the rest."

Four years later, Scot was commissioned Lieutenant in the United States Air Force and selected for pilot training. His first assignment was at Whiteman Air Force Base in Missouri while he waited to attend pilot training. Soon, he went off to pilot training at Laughlin Air Force Base in Del Rio, TX and earned his wings after a truly demanding year. Upon graduation he was assigned to Fairchild Air Force Base in Spokane, Washington flying the KC-135 Stratotanker. It is here where he deployed four times and defended the nation following the tragic attack on the nation during September 11th, 2001.

"I've traveled and deployed to many locations in the tanker, but mostly flew in support of missions over Iraq and Afghanistan. There was no place in the world we couldn't reach. In 2004, I was chosen as one of only six pilots who moved from flying tankers to flying airlift aircraft." Scot flew the

C-17 Globemaster III, the world's most advanced cargo plane. "You'd get orders in the morning to fly a combat mission and by evening you're flying a humanitarian mission, helping those in need. I truly loved the variety of it all." After nearly 10 years of heavy flying, it was time for Scot to be molded into the leader he was destined to become.

In 2008, he attended the U.S. Army's Command and General Staff and earning the title of "Jedi" as a graduate of the elite School of Advanced Military Studies. Following school, he served at the Pentagon where he spent two years on the Joint Staff working for the Chairman of the Joint Chiefs of Staff as a strategic planner in the Iraq Division. Then in 2012, he received his dream assignment, commanding a combat-ready squadron of KC-135 tankers. "I really fell in love with leadership at that point and knew I wanted more leadership opportunities like this." After command, Scot was selected for another year of school at the Naval War College in Newport, Rhode Island, followed by selection as the Vice Commander of Fairchild Air Force Base and then ultimately, Wing Commander of Scott AFB near Shiloh, Illinois serving and supporting over 14,000 personnel." As his solo act, Scot served as Vice Commander of 18th Air Force, an organization that serves over 36,000.

## THE TRANSITION

Scot decided to make his final landing and retired in the Fall of 2022 and started his coaching, training, speaking, and consulting business called 'Elevating Others'. "During my time as a base commander, I had a pretty serious medical condition that popped up out of nowhere." After a rear-end, car accident in December 2018, Scot sustained a moderate whiplash injury. "After an MRI scan of my neck, doctors noticed a sizeable brain tumor. I had yet to feel any effects from it, but a year later, the right side of my face went numb, I lost dexterity in my left hand, and began to walk with a slight limp. It was time to act."

In February 2020, Scot underwent a nearly 11-hour brain surgery to remove the tumor. "I gave up command of the base to my Deputy while I re-learned over the next four months how to do the basics again: walk, talk, see, and speak." During one of his many therapy walks, he passed by his 4-Star Commander in her car. "Most of the commanders and staff leadership live in the same neighborhood so there's no place to hide as the base commander. There I was, with my walker and an eye patch. She stopped and asked how I was doing." Always the optimist, Scot said he was doing great and asked if he could come back to work in a couple weeks. "She looked me square and the eye and said, 'What are you talking about?' I regretted asking as soon as she looked at me. She continued and said, 'I am not about to let you take the new transmission out and blow it. I will tell you when you can come back to work." Scot learned a valuable lesson that day. No matter who you are, we all deserve time to heal. And that's what he did. Later that fall he endured 30 rounds of radiation, all while serving the men and women of the base he loved.

Prior to retirement, there was a lot on Scot's mind wondering whether to stay in or step away. He thought about health and well-being. He thought about his autistic son, who was going into his senior year in high school and then off to college. He thought about the pros and cons of another assignment, another potential promotion, and another move. "The voice in my head was saying, 'You've done enough and now it's time to serve in a broader sense.' The timing felt right to transition and retire and I'm ready to take a new journey."

It didn't take long for Scot to transition. "Once I made up my mind, I had a pretty clear purpose in front of me. It had to involve elevating others and growing leaders in some way. I always loved teaching, coaching, and speaking. I get inspired by the 'a-ha' moments in others and want to help others succeed. I thought, you know what? God is telling me to build a business and fulfill my purpose. I just needed to learn and understand how to do this by building out my network."

Scot has built a solid network on LinkedIn and has been for over 15 years. "It's a tool, but a very powerful one if wielded properly. But I have to say, Gary Vaynerchuk was a major catalyst in my life for using tools like LinkedIn, Facebook, Instagram, etc., to build my personal brand and network. Following a disruptor like Gary Vee taught me the value of communicating across a variety of means and using content and connections to my advantage, both online and offline to build great relationships. To this day, my non-military network has quadrupled compared to my military network, only because I opened myself up to the world, being vulnerable to what I don't know and learning from experts, and exploiting these networking sites for what they are best designed and built to do." He continues, "I never really thought I would serve and lead beyond 10-12 years in the Air Force. Definitely not 25 years. What a journey!"

## LESSONS LEARNED

Be Present, Be Bold, Be Innovative

## WHAT'S NEXT

Scot's mission in life is simple: to inspire CEOs to front-line leaders to 'command with courage' so they can unleash the force within their team, ignite their innovation and skyrocket their bottom line. "If there's an organizational or leadership pain point, I like to help people overcome it so they can perform at a higher level. I also like speaking to veterans about utilizing their military education and experiences as a foundational advantage in civilian life. There is so much value veterans bring to the table."

Scot's expertise continues to climb like a rocket ship. Beyond his business, he's an independent facilitator for two leadership and development companies and one of the top emotional intelligence companies in the world. Through his business, Elevating Others, he delivers a variety of leadership and development programs to local government agencies and organizations, companies, and academia. "I'm often called upon to deliver motivational talks and keynotes for a variety of organizations, events, conferences, and podcasts. For the individual, I also provide one-on-one, executive coaching and leadership assessments. In 2023, I was chosen to be an Adjunct Faculty Member for the David Novak Leadership Institute at the University of Missouri and serve on the board for Soulcial Solutions, aimed at fighting food insecurity throughout the United States."

## THE MILITARY EFFECT

"Many transitioning Veterans want to find ways to continue serving. I've seen first-hand, large organizations like the ones I've been a part of, fail to grow, evolve, and retain membership because they often don't provide what a veteran yearns to have. Organizations, ask yourself, are you tapping into these Veteran needs and superpowers If you want to be Veteran friendly are you open to changing and adapting a bit to meet them halfway or are you just asking them to conform? Lean into your Veteran talent, sit them down and ask them their opinions, get to know them as a person and not just a military hire. Get to know them beyond what you read on a resume. They know a heck of a lot. Yeah, there may be some translation issues, but those are minor. Just know, they want to serve, feel valued and take action!" Scot believes in looking for ways to create an environment that is mutually beneficial for the organization and its Veteran employees, members, or volunteers that truly harnesses the power and value a Veteran brings to the table. This is the best way to obtain the highest level of organizational success."

# 17

## JAMES "BART" BARTELLONI, NAVY

linkedin.com/in/james-bart-bartelloni
**Hometown:** *Fairfax, Virginia*
**Currently Resides:** *San Diego, California*

## WHY I SERVED

Bart came from a family of veterans. His dad was in WWII, and his grandfather fought in WWI. A second-generation Italian immigrant, he was the only child to join (of three brothers and one sister). Recruited to play basketball and soccer at The Naval Academy, Bart never thought growing up he would fly or, ultimately, play Rugby in college. (He figured out, quickly, he was a division III athlete in a division I world.) Top Gun had just been released as he was entering the Academy and Naval Aviation was extremely exciting. This, no doubt, impacted his decision.

"The first day at the Naval Academy you read "Message to Garcia". It's literally sitting there on your bed. It's the first thing ingrained in your mind. Says Bart, "The moral of the story is this guy, he had to fulfill his mission. He did everything he could ever do, kicking and scratching. Take the initiative and face challenges directly. I brought this theme to my time in the cockpit: "Excellence takes preparation and an unrelenting drive."

Bart had to know everything about the jet. "We learned about the engine's hydraulics, the electronic systems, the environmental control systems, the weapons systems, everything. You had to be an expert at everything."

TOPGUN was the 1% of the 1%. It was the best of the best. "There was no trophy, there was no competition between us. Going through the class you want to be the best, but not by screwing over one of the other guys or doing something unsafe to win." Bart was driven to be the best. "A majority of the students and instructors played sports and are hyper competitive. Sports, especially team sports, are the breeding ground for excellence and discipline."

"Our air-to-air training was 1v1. You go from 1 versus 1, to 2 versus 2, to 4 versus 4, then you go 4 versus x. The graduation strike was something like 8v20. And oh, by the way, the 20, they get to regenerate. Or when you hit 20, they get replaced so it's more like 8v40." Everything was debriefed. The overarching theme of TOPGUN is a 'commitment to excellence'."

Even on the aircraft carrier everything was tracked. The ready room had a "greenie" board. "It tracked and graded successful landings and that's a huge deal. It added a competitive nature to the landings, and, in the end, the numbers don't lie." Every landing was graded then added to the main board in the back of the room. " You are listed by name in line periods, which are usually about three to four weeks long. The goal was to get the 30-40 blocks all green. No reds, no yellows." The results were there for everyone to see.

"Many people have multiple reasons for joining the Armed Forces. In the end, it is always the *people* you serve with that make being part of the military so special. Yes, you can become deeply involved in the geo-political reasons for this or that mission but in the end, you simply want to be your best for that man or women next to you. That is the special sauce of military service and, ultimately, without even knowing it, the subconscious reason I joined and thrived."

# THE TRANSITION

At the 10-year point, the Navy wanted to send Bart to War College. "I had no desire to get out of the cockpit. I'll never forget when I made the decision to get out. I was literally on a pinky landing, which means it's just about sunset." The landings are methodical, with each pilot being marshaled 20 miles behind the ship. "We're literally going down the 'shoot'. It's like an elevator and everyone has a push time." He continues, "I was about 10 miles behind the ship, looked around and said.... I'm done". It was time to get out. "The decision had been weighing on my mind for a while. At this crucial point in your military career, I believe everyone takes a serious look at continuing for a career or not. Ultimately, know this sounds crazy, but flying fighters off aircraft carriers had become boring."

"I wanted to get as far away from the military as possible.". For Bart, it no longer defined him. His first job was selling internet, e-business, mobile, telecommunication research for a company called Yankee Group. "It was 2002, and I'd walk into these offices and there'd be seats and cubicles. It was the beginning of the telecommunications bust. I didn't understand that. I've been out on aircraft carriers. I am kind of like, where the hell is everybody?"

Bart then helped to start a virtual reality software company with some key relationships. "We created the first ever military spec USB HOTAS (hands on throttle stick) game controls - I didn't know anything about this industry. Nothing". The company quickly sold, and Bart stepped into consulting, with a focus on strategic planning. "It was at this point, around the 5-year point of my transition, that the wheels almost fell off."

"I look back on it now and I was lost. Too egotistically bound by the persona that I had created over those 10-12 years to ask anyone for help. " It was the biggest business mistake Bart made. "I thought I was invincible, and I quickly learned, through multiple business failures and the loss of 100K's of thousands of dollars, that I am certainly not. I struggled financially and personally for years. All because of the ego." He continues, "For those making the transition, at any year point, seek mentorship and be honest with your goals and the obstacles that might hinder reaching those goals – financial, mental – just lay it all out on the table. Trust me, your transition will be MUCH smoother than mine ever was. Ultimately, the best way to accomplish this goal - NETWORK."

"I've been in health care, software technology, financial services and government consulting, it's all the same." Based on his TOPGUN naval aviation training, Bart looks at business from a bigger picture strategic perspective and had a keen ability to connect dots and see where a market is going or where partners/customers real driving business need resides. "I've always aggregated to business development. In a sales situation, I was talking to a guy who had a PhD in chemistry. There's no way I'd ever be able to talk to him at his level of knowledge, but I saw on his Twitter that he was a surfer and I'm a surfer and I instantly had credibility. From that point, just like funneling into a target area, I can begin to connect and drive the conversation toward the desired outcome: aligning their business needs with the abilities of your product or service. The key to the entire meeting was surfing. The only way to be successful in these situations is to 1/ take on the mindset taught in "Message to Garcia" and 2/ relentlessly research and prepare for a meeting like you would going into a defended target area. You must PREPARE."

## LESSONS LEARNED

There's always a way (with honor too)

## WHAT'S NEXT

Bart enjoys people. People are at the heart of business. "I enjoy meeting people, connecting with them on issues outside of business. Who is this person? What makes them tick? Outside of business, is there anything I can do for them on a 'human-to-human' basis? For that reason, I don't think I'll ever 'retire' or leave the business world completely. It's just too much fun."

Later in life, Bart picked up Stand Up Paddle Board (SUP) Surfing. A sport which changed his life. "I had never surfed or been on a SUP. I was so bad that my son and wife actually walked away from me as I was trying (operative word) to just stand on the SUP. OBTW, it was totally flat water." Fast forward a few years and Bart has SUP surfed Maldives, Mexico and, along with his partners, started a non-profit www.thesupvets.org . "There is no way to describe the spiritual power of surfing. Without knowing it, I took that first short story, Message to Garcia, and applied it to my surfing. I went out in any condition. It took me a year to catch my first wave." Since its founding in 2018, the SUP Vets has put over 50+ Veterans through their retreats. "Our retreats are very powerful. They are simple in design but deliberate in action." Bart says they are designed to create a space for sharing and camaraderie. "There is power in simplicity. A vast majority of our attendees are combat veterans who have been poked, prodded, screened, evaluated, etc. We don't do any of that." The retreats are designed to bring veterans together to just be present. "Whatever happens down there, whatever they feel like sharing is never forced."

Ultimately, Bart will continue supporting companies with business development and strategic excellence and continue to build his non-profit for the betterment and enjoyment of his fellow men and women veterans.

## THE MILITARY EFFECT

"When you're able to take everything you learn, into the military, put it into your great brain translator and translate it to business you will find success. You will also realize the amazing opportunities that exist in the civilian world. Consider the army platoon leaders sitting in a hut in Afghanistan, attempting to persuade local warlord leaders to assist them against the Taliban, despite the risk of being targeted by the Taliban for doing so. If such individuals, who navigate complex communication and leadership challenges in extreme situations, can't transition into successful business roles, then we are failing to adequately support them. After all, the primary barrier is often just a matter of adapting to different languages and communication styles. Too often, the insights of successful business executive veterans are disregarded simply because they lack a little communication ability and understanding of the business environment but, ultimately, understand how to solve the situation."

# 18

## JOE MUSSELMAN, NAVY

linkedin.com/in/joemusselman
**Hometown:** *Chicago, Illinois*
**Currently Resides:** *Chicago, Illinois*

## WHY I SERVED

The 20th member of his family to serve in the military, Joe's family first arrived in the United States in 1673 . "My sixth great grandfather came here from Bavaria then, and his son, Christian Besseler Musselman, ended up serving in '75 and '76. He wintered in Valley Forge with George Washington and Alexander Hamilton during the Revolutionary War." Joe had family members who fought at the Alamo, and other early revolutionary conflicts of our nation. "Growing up, I saw every uniform of every branch in every home." It was not a matter of if, it was a matter of when Joe would serve.

Entering college, Joe's uncle served as a shock trauma surgeon at Marine Special Operations Command. "At one point in time, he was the oldest deployed combat physician and medic in Operation Iraqi Freedom and Enduring Freedom." While traveling abroad in 2005 & 2006 for Joe's senior thesis project, he visited forward operating bases in Afghanistan & Iraq. "It was there I met a Navy Seal for the first time. When I arrived home, I withdrew my OCS package to the United States Marine Corps and enlisted in the United States Navy. I think my grandfather, who served as a Marine in WWII, turned in his grave."

Preparing for his basic training, Joe started training and entered 12 Ironman races to be ready. "It was important to do this. I was going to BUDS(basic underwater demolition school), and then hopefully SQT(seal qualification training) and needed to be ready mentally." He knew the challenge ahead would only be met with fierce preparation. After several competitions, including some 50-mile runs, Joe went in September 2010.

## THE TRANSITION

After a lifetime of family service, two years of preparation, meeting members of the SOF, reading books and history, and finally making it to BUDS training, he was injured badly. "If you want to make God laugh, tell him about your plans. I suffered a spine injury and spent the next 8 months in Coronado going through rehab". Joe says, "It was a reorientation towards what I was always meant to do. I just didn't know it at the time". He recognized during this time in rehab that members of the community were not certain about the next steps once they transitioned from their military service to their next great adventure in life.

Despite his injury, he had to prove to himself and the community he loved that he could still add value. Joe launched a Listening tour in 2013, interviewing 215 Navy Seals & special operators across 7 states in six months. He asked each member the same set of questions, starting with, 'What happens to SEALS after they became SEALS?'. No one had a good answer. "I spent my entire life savings at that point. My girlfriend at the time thought I was insane. However now she is my wife and expecting our 3rd child."

From this effort, The Honor Foundation(THF) was born. "At THF, we set out to fiercely empathize with the Special Operations Forces (SOF) community during their time of transition. No one accomplished this effectively with programs to match. Our curriculum was crafted by the community, for the community." Former SOF operators and spouses are now employees and volunteers for the mission. "We have a broader community of support that spans 10,000 plus. The SOF community values are interwoven into the very fabric of our organization. Our team holds ourselves to the same standards of excellence because we understand them, live and hopefully lead by example. The vision of the organization is clear: we imagine a world where 65,000 members of the Special Operations Forces community experience a seamless transition. Our mission: to serve others with honor, for life." Their next mission is clear and continues to impact the world, remaining the true north star. Now in 2024, in its 10th anniversary, The Honor Foundation has supported nearly 4,000 operators and their families through a 12-week program across nine campuses.

Joe left in February of 2019, passing the reigns over to a former Navy Seal, Capt. Ret.,Matt Stevens. "His reputation in the Teams was exceptional. He had served on THF's board of directors, and we as a board understood his ability to advocate for people. He was ready for a new mission." Understanding the mission to be steady hands, Joe quickly began to embark on his next journey, launching his first early-stage venture capital fund in Silicon Valley. 'I was blessed to have early inspiration in this sector from an early mentor, Kevin Compton, who made an amazing impact on my life. As one of the most successful executives in the industry, he became my example to follow." Currently, Joe is on to his second fund which is a nine-figure strategy. It brings him back to his professional roots, focusing on National Security Technology in support of the Special Operations and broader Defense communities. "If you believe in who you are serving, it's easy to be persistent, remain inspired, and execute."

## LESSONS LEARNED

Have a clear vision – Craft your mission or worthy cause – Understand your values - Formulate your plan – Execute.

## WHAT'S NEXT

His next thesis is focused. "I want to serve mission-first founders on the national security of the United States and our allies globally. These personalities are closest to a Navy SEAL or Special Operator."

Although Joe left the board of Directors of the Honor Foundation in 2021, he continues to fundraise. His new goal for the institution is to build The Honor For Life Foundation, a one-hundred-million-dollar effort which will continue to serve THF in perpetuity.

His new career in venture capital takes up nearly ninety percent of Joe's time. Investing in extraordinary teams, leaders, and cultures and supporting them to execute on their mission effectively, he is incredibly detail-oriented around the distribution of his focus as a resource.

His firm (BVVC) represents a body of his work gathered over the last decade. "My podcast is called the TLC Equation. It's a show that examines and explores fundamental truths surrounding the greatest Teams, Leaders, and Cultures (TLC) on earth". This allows Joe the opportunity to scale his listening tours with high-value conversations to a much wider audience.

## THE MILITARY EFFECT

At some point, every veteran will need to transition, it's guaranteed. Joe understands that many ask themselves the same question, "What's next?". His advice is, "Find someone who inspires you. When you start with a 'who', it becomes much more exciting for those in transition."

# 19

## JOHN KEATING, ARMY

linkedin.com/in/john-keating-5795694
**Hometown:** *Tahoe, California*
**Currently Resides:** *Frisco, Texas*

### WHY I SERVED

Born in a Catholic Charities orphanage in Los Angeles with a club foot, John was adopted several weeks after his birth by parents who found a doctor to correct John's foot. Growing up in the Sierra Nevada mountains, John learned to ski as he learned to walk. Summer months were spent swimming and sailing at Tahoe where the water temp is usually below 70 degrees Fahrenheit. Like most children of the 70's, John grew up in the analog world of black & white TV, with no video games or internet, and one rotary dial phone in the kitchen.

"Graduating high school with average grades and no money, I had few options. Stay in a resort town and work in hospitality for minimum wage and tips, or get out and see the world, learn new skills, and save money for college." Those who knew John weren't surprised when he joined the military.

"It was 1982, and I was literally pumping gas for tips. Reagan was President, but the economy was still stalled, and jobs were hard to come by. I walked to the local fire station and picked up a block of free government cheese, and thought, this is the only handout I will ever take. I signed up to go into Army Aviation, hoping to one day go to flight school and be a helicopter pilot."

John went to Basic Training at Fort Jackson, SC, and Advanced Training (AIT) at Fort Eustis, VA for Helicopter Weapons Systems (68J), and was assigned to the 268th Attack Helicopter Battalion, 9th Cavalry Brigade at Fort Lewis, WA. "I Corps had been reactivated and was affectionately known as the 'Toys R Us' Division, as we received all the latest equipment to be tested before contracting by the Army. Our orders were to 'use it, abuse it, try and break it, but don't lose it.' The catch was, anytime you broke something, you had to write a report."

Transitioning to military intelligence, John graduated at the top of his Counterintelligence Agent (97B) class and deployed to Korea, where he was assigned to the Camp Red Cloud (Uijeongbu) Field Office, as part of the 209th MI Company, 524th MI Battalion. John completed his associate degree with Central Texas College and taught Law Enforcement classes for the MPs (Military Police) at Camp Liberty Bell and Camp Bonifas along the DMZ, where civilian instructors weren't allowed.

After spending 15 months in Korea, John returned to the US and was assigned to the 902d MI Group at Fort Meade, MD. "I volunteered to go and was assigned to the 164th MI Company, 513th MI Battalion at Fort Monmouth, NJ, and was in Saudi Arabia before the end of the month. Shortly after the liberation of Kuwait, John returned to Fort Meade, MD, and was immediately recruited to serve on another SAP, this time in support of DELTA ("Special Operations Task Force") as a counterintelligence asset, providing what John describes as, "non-traditional support."

## THE TRANSITION

After 13-years of active duty in the Army, three Military Occupational Specialties (MOS), a Top-Secret security clearance, two overseas assignments, a combat tour, and a letter of acceptance to Warrant Officer Candidate School, John made the difficult decision to leave the military to finish his college degree, start a business, and to one day have a family of his own. Over the next five years he would graduate from Towson University, open a multi-state financial services company for tech start-ups, get married, buy a house, have two sons, and move to Texas.

With his sons in school, John ran for city council and won his first election in 2010. Once elected, John went to work on several of Frisco's most important projects, including the Dallas Cowboys partnership at The Star, moving the National Soccer Hall of Fame to Frisco with FC Dallas, opening the University of North Texas Frisco campus, renewing the NCAA Division 1 Football Championship contract with Frisco, building a new state-of-the-art library, and bringing the PGA Headquarters to Frisco.

## LESSONS LEARNED

"Changing how we perceive ourselves changes the way we perceive others. As our self-image improves, our relationships, our job performance, and everything else we do moves in a more positive direction. How you show up for yourself is critical! Continue to build your identity and your brand. Be the person in the room someone wants to meet!"

## WHAT'S NEXT

"In 2010 I reluctantly joined the VFW, thinking I don't need another meeting, and I don't want to sit around drinking beer, smoking cigarettes and telling war stories. I was surprised to find fellow members like me who were home now and wanted to continue serving their country by serving their community. They wanted a mission outside of family and work, where we spoke the same language and understood the value of military service and camaraderie."

John's career in the military was spent focused on specific time-sensitive classified missions, operating either independently or on small 2-man teams as part of compartmentalized special units.

"My VFW family was a microcosm of the military with all branches represented. It was fascinating to hear where people were stationed and what their mission was, while at the same time I was somewhere else, doing something else. We were all working towards the same goal, the same positive outcome, on the same team, without ever knowing each other."

John recently purchased a lot in Frisco and is building a new home, a great metaphor for this stage of his life. He celebrated his 60th birthday in September with family and friends. John earned his real estate license this summer and ran his first "Spartan Race" (6 miles with 25 obstacles) in the fall. John is running for his third and final term on Frisco city council as this book is being written, with Election Day on 4 May 2024.

## THE MILITARY EFFECT

"The mayor tasked me with making Frisco 'veteran friendly and veteran ready.' This meant more than just extending a warm welcome to our veteran families; it entailed actively seeking or generating opportunities for their success. Our Frisco Veterans Advisory Committee had outlined several crucial projects, including the revitalization of the Veterans Memorial at Frisco Commons Park where new plaques and benches were installed, landscaping was replaced, and a solemn centerpiece known as a 'Soldiers Cross' was added. We also collaborated to have Frisco designated a Purple Heart City, which inspired other veterans to construct a Gold Star Family Memorial here, as envisioned by Medal of Honor Recipient Hershel "Woody" Williams.

# 20

## JULIANA MERCER, MARINES

linkedin.com/in/julianamercer
**Hometown:** *San Diego, California*
**Currently Resides:** *San Diego, California*

## WHY I SERVED

"I never intended to join the military, much less the Marine Corps." In her senior year of high school, Juliana had a track scholarship for college. She was excited to go. "One day I was in a strip mall in my small town and all of the recruiting offices were lined up in a row. I had zero intention of joining but was bored and wanted to learn what the military was all about."

"The last office was Marine Corps, and I didn't know what a Marine was." The recruiter told Juliana what a Marine was and what it would take to become one of 'the few, the proud'. "They talked about learning to be a leader from day one, service to your country and to others, and how difficult it was to become a Marine physically, mentally and emotionally." The challenge resonated with Juliana. "Everything the recruiter told me a Marine was, was something I wanted to be. So, before I left the office, I signed the paperwork and started the process of going to boot camp."

Juliana's parents were not thrilled. "When I told the news to them, my mom started crying and my dad just–shook his head at me." But their view changed, and soon her parents became her biggest supporters. "I graduated from boot camp a couple of weeks before 9/11. My entire 20s and 30s our country was at war, I was at war, my friends were at war."

"When we were deployed, my job was civil affairs. It was basically a nonprofit that was working in combat zones. We were paying reparations to families and businesses that had damage caused by the war that was going on in their communities. So, I got to serve others in a capacity beyond being just a Marine." Juliana's time in the service lasted almost sixteen years, with ten of them active duty.

## THE TRANSITION

Between deployments to Iraq and Afghanistan, Juliana spent almost five years working with the wounded population in a unit called Marine for Life. "We were a Wounded Warrior battalion and the liaison team that took care of our wounded coming back from Iraq and Afghanistan." Juliana found herself in a place doing purposeful work but feeling purposeless.

"I had accumulated this wealth of knowledge and subject matter expertise in supporting a transitioning warfighter. I worked on things like employment, education, community and social engagement." Juliana continues, "I helped the veterans, and their family members reintegrate and connect to purposeful work or community. We helped guide them to find the right education as well."

But the culmination of all the collected trauma, grief, pain, and loss on her own became too much. "All of the wounded that I worked with, the family members that suffered, the suicides that were happening at home, just all piled up on me. I couldn't see myself continuing to work In the state that I was in. I felt guilty because I had the subject matter expertise and so many people needed help and it was hard for me to step away. It got to a point where it just wasn't the right thing for me anymore. Emotionally and spiritually, I couldn't continue being at war."

Juliana pursued talk therapy shortly after. "I knew that I needed help, and I didn't want to get on a bunch of anti-depressants. Around that same time, I met an organization that sent veterans to receive psychedelic assistive therapy in other countries where it's not illegal (Costa Rica, Mexico, Peru, etc.). I ended up going on a retreat with them. It changed my life."

The authentic, joyful, and loving Juliana returned. "That morning, I knew that I needed to do everything I could to help veterans connect to these life-saving treatments. I got really active with Heroic Hearts Project, helping them to advocate. I became a coach to help veterans through their psychedelic journey and eventually through my vocal advocacy was connected to the organization that I work for now, Healing Breakthrough, where I advocate for access to MDMA-Assisted Therapy for veterans through the VA."

## LESSONS LEARNED

Balance comes in making sure that my work isn't the only thing that I'm doing.

## WHAT'S NEXT

"I am now working on the advocacy side on Capitol Hill, talking to our legislators about the need for the VA to set up a program and be able to deliver MDMA assisted therapy as soon as FDA approved. We will soon have this solution that's going to be medically available here in the US, so veterans don't have to leave the country. We're seeing this as kind of the light at the end of the tunnel and the first novel treatments to actually start saving the sunlight."

Juliana continues to work strategically with the VA. "They are the largest mental health care provider in the nation. If we can help them be successful at rolling out this therapy, it's going to be a model for other healthcare systems. It's also helping to de-stigmatize and create awareness."

Her sole mission now is getting DMA therapy successfully into the hands of as many veterans that need it. "I want to help make an impact and get that accomplished. It's really such a huge potential for impact. I'm very optimistic about what this is going to be able to do for our veteran community and our nation." For Juliana, this is her life.

## THE MILITARY EFFECT

"Regarding transition, I think the biggest piece of advice I can give is don't do it by yourself. Don't think that you know what you're talking about because you don't. This is something that you've never done before and it's not an easy process. If you do it alone, it can take you many times to figure it out and you might fail when you don't have. Get the support that you need."

# 21

## JULIANA VIDA, NAVY

linkedin.com/in/julianavida
**Hometown:** *Lancaster, Pennsylvania*
**Currently Resides:** *Reston, Virginia*

## WHY I SERVED

An identical twin, Julie has always seen life from a different perspective. "We grew up in Amish country in Lancaster, Pennsylvania. Both of us were on the path to college, but the family didn't have the resources to pay for our education." One day her twin sister Marie came home saying, "I just joined the Navy, and you should apply!" The idea didn't really interest Julie, as she hadn't known anyone growing up who had plans to join the military and had a negative (and uninformed) view of high school classmates who were headed into the Service.

Marie explained the job she was enlisting to do was a cryptologic technician (interpretive), better known as a linguist. "That intrigued me because I enjoyed foreign languages and had an aptitude for Spanish." They joined the Navy together, going through Naval boot camp in the same Company, starting the basic Russian course at Defense Language Institute in the same class, and even rooming together in barracks.

Julie excelled, graduating at the top of her class, and gaining acceptance into an intermediate program for another year. "During that second year, a career counselor encouraged me to apply to the US Naval Academy. I initially rejected the idea not feeling I could compete with (what she wrongly assumed was) a pool of top academic students."

After more encouragement, she submitted an application and got in 'direct', not having to go to Navy prep school first. It was the start of a 22-year career. Says Julie, " I went into the Navy to be a linguist. Thought I was going to be a spy, or an attaché, or something cool." She had no idea the cool factor would come her way, but not how she expected. The year she graduated from Annapolis; Congress lifted the combat restriction that prevented women to go into combat roles. "My class was the first one to have the opportunity to go fly jets, the full range of helicopter types, and to serve on combatant ships." That stroke of luck and timing made all the difference.

Traveling the world, Julie was deployed five times, including USS Peleliu(L-HA-5) when 9/11 happened. She also deployed on USS Barry(DDG-52), USS Theodore Roosevelt(CVN-71), and twice USS Nimitz(CVN-68). Her career saw both sides, as a surface warfare officer before transitioning to aviation as a helicopter pilot. "It was a time when the Navy was 'undermanned. They needed officers to stay in.I was married at the time to a classmate, and we both asked to transition from surface warfare to naval aviation. If not approved, we would both have got out." The Navy approved the transition request. "That's how I became a helicopter pilot."

Near the end of her career, Julie got orders to the Pentagon. "If you stick around long enough, you will get orders to go to the Pentagon. I just happened to be assigned to the Office of Chief Information." At the time she knew nothing about IT. "I was there to support the senior executive along with a three-star Admiral. I had to learn really fast." There she pivoted into more tech focused roles. Says Julie, "It was fantastic, and a career I never could have architected for myself."

## THE TRANSITION

As Julie exited the military, she knew that some things had to be learned. "Fortunately, I was in DC, and there were lots of places for me to get the education I needed." One of them was the National Defense University. "With a few years of technology leadership under my belt, I knew I needed to bolster my knowledge in the industry."

With such a diverse working history, Julie has had to become adept in sharing her experience. "Let me talk to you about my career as an arc. There are themes you can pick from it, including open mindedness to try new things, learning fast by tapping into others' expertise and knowledge, and saying yes to opportunities others present. Because it's not obvious how I went from one thing to the other."

She has quickly become good at being her own brand ambassador at LinkedIn. "Now I have these extended networks and communities of people who like to talk about technology, cybersecurity, equality in the workplace, and the unique challenges women face." For Julie, LinkedIn has literally changed her life. "Connecting people is my superpower."

Julie's speaking career is evolving, slowly. "It will be a big part of my career when I leave corporate America. I have been fortunate enough to get in front of many companies like Hilton & Pepsi when speaking at various technology conferences." But there she doesn't talk about technology, and instead focuses on building confidence and learning from failure. It's what her first book will be about.

## LESSONS LEARNED

People will like you and trust you if you speak their language.

## WHAT'S NEXT

A quick learner, Julie has transitioned her career to be a person who can translate technical topics to people who don't have technical background. "I use storytelling. I use metaphors. I use little vignettes to kind of make technology real for people because not everybody needs to know all the ones and zeros of the tech stack. Most people don't have a strong technical background and just want the wave tops and how to use it. They just need to know what's in it for them."

"I love to talk to people and learn from them. It's been an important part of building my network, upskilling myself, and getting to know the right people. I use social networks to elevate other people. And that's easy. just tag them. You know, if there's just a post about people who inspire you, I always tag somebody in there and I say, you inspire me because you did this for me, or I highlight something that someone did at work or a speech that they gave. It's so easy to do."

Julie believes that every day we wake up, we should be doing something good. "It makes the difference in somebody else's day. And that's how I look at the value of social networks because when other people view me as someone who helps other people, they trust me. People are hungry for feeling included and feeling important and feeling like someone cares about them."

A previous game show winner on both the Wheel of Fortune and The Weakest Link, Julie hopes to compete again. "I want to get on more game shows. I recently auditioned for one and was getting pretty close, then the writers' strike happened."

## THE MILITARY EFFECT

"Many of us go into a job looking on paper like we have little experience, with no certifications of any kind or formal education needed for the role. I've considered having my own business as a transition expert for women veterans because there aren't a lot of unique specific resources for women to help them look past their gaps and focus on their strengths. Women need more of a boost because we often lack the executive sponsorship, access to opportunities, and influential decision makers 'looking out for us."

# 22

## KATHERINE ROWE, ARMY

linkedin.com/in/katherine-rowe
**Hometown:** *Multiple bases*
**Currently Resides:** *Austin, Texas*

## WHY I SERVED

When Katherine started looking at colleges, entering the military was the furthest thing from her mind. A competitive field hockey player, her focus was to earn an athletic scholarship. "My dad was a 30-year veteran. We visited West Point. It just didn't resonate with me at the time." She landed a scholarship at Lindenwood University but had a devastating knee injury that sent her home soon after.

Being home for six months recovering, Katherine had a lot of time to reflect and really thought deeply about what she wanted to do. "I had this negative connotation with the military. We moved around so much, and I never had a hometown experience." She continues, "Service was just so important to my family. My dad, my sister, my grandfather, my two brothers-in law. I was surrounded by a commitment to service, and realized it was my time to serve."

Katherine finished her college career at Clark University on a 3-year ROTC scholarship, commissioning into the Army after graduation. "I've always done things my own way. So, I ended up on the same path, but I did it a little differently." She did seven years of active duty and then a year of the reserves at grad school. "I actually taught ROTC at the University of Texas as a part time instructor."

## THE TRANSITION

On deployment in Korea, Katherine began to map her transition. "I knew I hit my commitment and thought it was probably time to get out. I also realized I just didn't have as much control over my personal life as I wanted." So, she talked to another peer at her officer level who had started applying to business school. "He didn't get in where he wanted so he was reapplying and helped me out. It really made me think about the path I hoped to take."

Katherine started to map her passions out. "It always came back to sports, entertainment, and stuff like that. Throughout growing up, moving around, and being deployed, I had seen how sports can transcend borders and language." She remembers one time while deployed on a Forward

Operating Base (FOB), several soldiers gathered to play a small soccer game with the Slovakian Army in the middle of the base. "I had seen the power of sports and how it connects people across the board. And so, I thought deep down that's where I wanted to be."

Her goal didn't come to fruition until business school where Katherine started to get exposed to a new set of opportunities. "In college I coached a player who had a job with the MLS. I just started to build this web of connections." She continues, "At the University of Texas our head of employer relations was also an Air Force veteran. She was also the faculty lead of the veteran's group for the MBA students." Katherine realized all her classmates were already going to consulting pre-MBA launch weeks and asked herself, 'Am I behind?' "She asked me what I wanted to do and told me that Nike was coming to campus. It turned out that a veteran was working there who had also been active in Service to School, where Katherine was currently volunteering."

That's where Katherine's network really came in, as she began to engage with industry mentors. "So, Kirk Goldsberry is a basketball analytics expert who I worked for at business school, who had previously been at the San Antonio Spurs and Grantland. He became a mentor of mine. Through Kirk, I met so many great people in sports, one of which is Rebecca Feferman who has been a publicist, strategist, and has done a lot with South by Southwest and other media organizations. Both told me from the beginning that I don't need to start from the bottom. I've got this."

## LESSONS LEARNED

Transition is a process, it's not like you snap your fingers and it's over.

## WHAT'S NEXT

Graduating from business school in 2020, Katherine had a work published on a sports industry website. It was still COVID, and the job market was tight, so she moved back home with her parents. With limited options she began to write a weekly newsletter about the business of sports. Her efforts soon began to pay off, and work started trickling in.

"I focused on building my portfolio and ended up getting hired by a consultancy group under the Kraft Group (owns the New England Patriots). Through that whole process that summer I met several veterans that worked in sports, or once did. I realized that we didn't have a place for people to turn to, whether it be just sort of like affinity across the industry, or to have candid conversations with people that have a similar background." Katherine created a LinkedIn group, Veterans in Sports, to provide more information to veterans getting out. "Last spring, we had a great gathering at the NFL Combine. My goal is to eventually turn it into a non-profit organization adding events and other formats to bring the community together."

Katherine loves to help others create a personal brand. "Everything I've done over the last three or four years has been mostly on LinkedIn. I really leaned into the platform, posting my work and building the brand. It's helped to create many relationships." She continues to work hard and curate the content. "I don't want something to be transactional. I want to get to know people and stay in touch with them and keep them updated on where I'm going and what I'm working on."

## THE MILITARY EFFECT

"I do think from a network effect, your veteran mentors and the veteran connections that you find are so helpful in the job search. I've always thought the main reason I got a role in the tech industry was because Jackie Yearney, the CMO, was a veteran and saw my potential. Others likely questioned my ability to do a role with limited civilian experience, but Jackie did, and I got hired."

# 23

## KIRSTEN CAMPBELL BRUNSON, ARMY

linkedin.com/in/kirstenbrunson
**Hometown:** *Largo, Maryland*
**Currently Resides:** *Joint Base Lewis McCord, Washington*

## WHY I SERVED

Kirsten always wanted to be a lawyer. After her freshman year in college at Hofstra University, she was home for the summer and saw the "Be all you can be" commercial on TV. "After that, I went down to the recruiting station and the only person there was the Army recruiter. He tried to get me to drop out of college and enlist." Instead, Kirsten signed up for ROTC, finished her degree, and joined the Army on an 8-year commitment.

Kirsten was commissioned as a military police officer, but she was aware of a program in the JAG Corps called The Funded Legal Education Program (FLEP) where the Army would send her to law school after a few years on active duty. She initially thought, "That's the way to go." At the last minute, she changed her mind and applied for a three-year educational delay, going to law school at her own expense with the understanding that she would apply to the JAG Corps upon completion.

Her first duty station was Germany. As soon as Kirsten hit the ground, a new friend immediately fixed her up with a soldier. Less than two years later, they got married. "He's Infantry, I'm JAG. We tended to complement each other, serving on large installations, and were stationed together a lot more than many married couples."

She served proudly for 23 years, finishing up her career as a military judge.

## THE TRANSITION

Kirsten always told herself, "I'll do this as long as I'm having a good time." She made it to the rank of Colonel and was stationed at Fort Bragg, NC while her husband was deployed. "I was assigned to the Military Commissions in DC. But then my husband was selected for General Officer and assigned to Fort Bragg." Kirsten decided it was time to retire. "I like my husband more than I like my job, and we are going to live together."

Enjoying a smooth transition to retirement, Kirsten tackled the challenge of education for her children. "My kids had gone to a Christian school, and it sort of fell apart around the time I was about to retire." She could not find another private or public school she was comfortable enrolling her child in. Says Kirsten, "I learned that there's a very large community of homeschoolers in and around Fayetteville, North Carolina." For three years, her youngest joined that community and Kirsten became a homeschool teacher.

Children's ministry also became a focus area for Kirsten. She managed the children's department of her church for several years. Kirsten also became involved with the Rick Herrema Foundation. "Rick was a Special Forces Soldier who was killed in action. His friends and family got together and started this project in Fayetteville, North Carolina. Basically, they wanted a green space for military families. " Kirsten helped with an annual event they hosted, which served as a fundraiser. "It was like the American Ninja Warrior Challenge. Soldiers and folks from the community came out and competed on this thing. It was fantastic."

## LESSONS LEARNED

If you tell people the truth, they have the information needed to make their decisions.

## WHAT'S NEXT

Unlike many retirees, Kirsten still has a child at home. She has three more years until her youngest finishes high school. Until then, much of her focus is on him and his activities, in which she is heavily involved. She attends all of her son's gymnastics meets and is a leader in his Scout troop. As her husband is still serving on active duty, she continues to serve the military community as a senior spouse. In addition, she chairs the Military and Veterans committee of the National Association of Women Judges and, as a member of the Military Justice Review Panel, will spend the next several years conducting a comprehensive review of the Uniform Code of Military Justice.

## THE MILITARY EFFECT

"My best advice is to take advantage of the transition resources. They are all free. Don't cut ties, use it as a springboard for what's next."

# 24

# LARISA HARRINGTON, AIR FORCE

linkedin.com/in/larisa-harrington-45687a160
**Hometown:** Woodbridge, Virginia
**Currently Resides:** New Market, Maryland

## WHY I SERVED

Growing up in a military family, Larisa spent every summer visiting her retired Army father still living in Germany. The summer before her senior year, with no interest in college, she worked as an intern for the Army. When she mentioned joining the military, the captain she was interning for said, "You are not cut out for the Army. You should consider the Air Force". Both of her parents agreed that the quality of life in the Air Force was a better fit for her than in the Army. So, Larisa took the Armed Services Vocational Aptitude Battery (ASVAB) and scored high enough to join the Air Force and specialize in military intelligence.

Her career started in linguistics. "I spoke French & German and felt this would be a cool job". Unfortunately, there was not a need for either of those languages, so Larisa was assigned to learn Farsi. While waiting for language school to start, someone dropped out of the Turkish class, and she was asked to change languages to learn Turkish instead. It was a perfect fit, as Ft Meade was the only base where she could be assigned. With her family nearby, Larisa couldn't be happier.

For eighteen of her twenty years of service, Larisa was stationed at Ft Meade (only broken up by a deployment and language training in California). She never loved her job as a linguist, but she loved serving her country and the amazing people she got to serve with. Throughout her career, she was blessed with great leaders & mentors.

## THE TRANSITION

Shortly after arriving at her first duty station, Larisa began working in health and wellness. "I'm not sure what the catalyst was, but I decided to get a part-time job at a gym after work." She fell in love with helping people improve their health and well-being and got certified as a personal trainer and yoga teacher. She continued working for a civilian gym and also began teaching fitness classes for military members. "I knew it's what I wanted to do." Over time, Larisa started learning more about mental, physical, and emotional health and became a certified life coach. "Honestly, I had no idea you could make money doing this."

After 16 years, Turkish linguists were no longer needed in the Air Force. "Because of my security clearance, there were not many opportunities for me to move elsewhere. I was fortunate to have been given the opportunity to have a special duty as a Readiness NCO to finish out my 20-year military career." That special duty allowed her to support the well-being of service members and their families, doing much of the same work she had been doing in her side job. She started her company while on active duty and intended to pursue it full-time after retirement, however, she was scared to give up a stable income and took a job at the National Institutes of Health to save some money before going all in with her business.

"In 2017, we moved to a new town, and built a house with a yoga retreat." Larisa immediately joined BNI (found out about it from Facebook) to force herself to talk to people about her business. "I was uncomfortable, but knew I had to do it." Ironically, it was the Pandemic that really jump-started things. "I was already doing virtual coaching, traveling lots to speak and train, and juggling mom duties." Her clients enjoyed doing yoga from home, and online teaching made it accessible for many more. "I started group coaching in addition to leading yoga online and we doubled our revenue."

## LESSONS LEARNED

Relationships matter. How you treat people matters.

## WHAT'S NEXT

As a mother to two school-aged children, Larisa enjoys the flexibility of doing much of her work virtually while also being able to travel to speak and train around the country. She still works for the Air Force Wounded Warriors, leading yoga and meditation to military members who have been wounded, ill or injured while serving. "For me, it's a great way to continue serving and to stay connected to the military community." She also leads virtual sessions each month and travels to wounded warrior in-person events throughout the year.

In her own company environment, Larisa continues to lead well-being and yoga sessions virtually for both individuals and organizations, as well as leads in-person retreats for leaders and executives. She is also preparing to launch a corporate leadership and well-being program to support successful professionals in expanding their impact without sacrificing their health or relationships.

## THE MILITARY EFFECT

"Hiring execs shouldn't put people into boxes. Veterans are team players, loyal and tenacious. There is so much more to them than what's written on the resume."

# 25

## LAURA NOEL, AIR FORCE

linkedin.com/in/laura-noel
**Hometown:** *Lancaster, Pennsylvania*
**Currently Resides:** *Nashua, New Hampshire*

### WHY I SERVED

Attending college in Millersville, Pennsylvania, Laura had no idea what direction her life was going in. While there she became aware of Army ROTC. "My friend got me into some classes, and I enjoyed it. There was a closeness of people and I felt cared for. It was a great community to learn from. It had a different vibe promoting positive discussions and service beyond us".

With encouragement from her dad, who was a Marine, she joined the Air Force. "I did a delayed enlistment and went to boot camp 11 months later. I definitely had a chip on my shoulder and was a bit edgy". Her adventurous spirit and desire to serve and explore the world lent to becoming a ground radio scope operator in a mobility unit and serving in Desert Shield/Desert Storm. Said Laura, "I had just turned 21 but felt like I was part of a new family."

There were opportunities to grow in any number of directions. "It's the only organization that I know of where you can completely change careers and your job path while still maintaining upward progression. With a love for music, Laura participated in an Air Force talent show that got her into a touring group through Air Force Entertainment, called Tops in Blue. While touring with Tops in Blue, she auditioned for and was accepted into the Air Force band and had the opportunity to serve and perform around the world. "We were part of the USAF public affairs missions and as such, performed everywhere from local schools to embassies in foreign countries, as well as for our troops in deployed locations."

Soon, Laura experienced another career change and became superintendent of the Honor Guard in New England. "It was so meaningful to perform funeral honors alongside the Air National Guard and Reserve units." Ironically, her first experience with military funeral honors was honoring her father. "It made it that much more meaningful and powerful when I got to serve in that way for other families who had lost a loved one."

Laura grappled with emotional strain and compassion fatigue, especially when interacting with bereaved families. "I was often talking to the families on the phone. They would want to share about their loved one and always asked if I would be there for the funeral service. It was an emotional connection." She showed every time knowing how meaningful it was to them.

Laura found solace and meaning in her duties, particularly during commemorative events like Memorial Day. "I remember being involved in an event at the State House in Boston on Memorial Day. It was so meaningful and beautiful to honor those who had served and made the ultimate sacrifice." These experiences taught her valuable lessons about integrity, teamwork and building meaningful relationships.

## THE TRANSITION

Nearing the end of her service, Laura became a leadership school Commandant where she led a team of instructors who taught leadership skills to first- and second-line supervisors. Not knowing what she wanted to do beyond that, as she approached almost 27 years of service, it slowly became clear. "I had collected degrees over the years, and had lots of experience coaching, facilitating and teaching leadership skills." She knew it was something she wanted to pursue after active duty. "These critical skills helped me become the entrepreneur I am today."

Laura had no idea how to start or grow a business. "Someone helped set up LinkedIn in 2017, as it wasn't a priority previously. I sought mentorship in the coaching and marketing spaces and really invested in my growth. Learning from that investment in myself paid huge dividends." A former Chief Master Sergeant (top 1% in the Air Force), she had no intention of approaching anyone in service to become her first clients. "I found myself thinking, 'How am I going to make this happen if I feel it's a conflict of interest in my military network?'" Laura focused on the end result and what she wanted. "The resources came around me to make it happen. I attracted people, organizations and potential clients who were looking for the coaching I was offering."

## LESSONS LEARNED

"Being an exceptional leader means you also have to be willing to be an intelligent follower. You don't want to be the smartest person in the room. Surround yourself with people who know more than you, so you can grow. And you can only grow as far as your level of awareness will take you. Seeking mentorship is critical for success."

## WHAT'S NEXT

Her business has been in operation since 2017, and she is now pivoting her focus while completing her PhD in Organizational Leadership Psychology. "I feel like I am a kid just starting over again, and it's exciting!". Laura now does speaking engagements, keynotes and workshops for some non-profits, corporations, and military clients. "My focus is on leadership and mindset. It's so wonderful and cool to go back 'home' to the various military bases and facilitate these classes and sessions."

Laura sees herself doing more consulting. "I have a background in organizational psychology and development and am currently working with a consulting firm working with generative AI. I am also immersed in quantitative research and analysis on the subject of Intuition and Decision. I feel grateful because many of the opportunities I find myself working towards have come from my networks and relationships developed with others over the years."

"Networking was highly encouraged while I was active. We had the airmen's group and others focused on non-profit activities." Laura stays involved with The Air Force Sergeants Association & the Air Force Association. "There are chapters all over the country. Sometimes I'll attend and sing the National Anthem." She has also started participating in professional networks such as the Society for Industrial and Organizational Psychology(SIOP), the International Coaching Federation(ICF), and other speaker and facilitator networks.

"My hope is to also develop CEU modules for organizations focused on leadership." Author of *Rat Race Robot* , Laura has a goal to one day be a TEDx speaker. "For me, failure is not an option! We only fail when we decide to quit ourselves. Falling down and making mistakes is a part of learning. It's an essential part of the growth process."

## THE MILITARY EFFECT

"Many don't know that band is a career field. We deploy. We perform with the troops at home and abroad. We help to build camaraderie." Many have advanced degrees, and some even hold doctorates in music. "It's a full-time thing. The band is important for recruiting and public affairs." Laura continues, " A town or school may not want a military presence, but they will welcome a band because music connects people, brings them together and fosters goodwill. It also helps shift perceptions of who Americans are. This connection humanizes people and helps them to find common ground."

## 26

# LINDSEY STREETER, ARMY

linkedin.com/in/lindsey-streeter-345aa22a
**Hometown:** *Washington, D.C.*
**Currently Resides:** *Richmond Hill, Georgia*

## WHY I SERVED

Lindsey always wanted to play football and go to college. "I came to the harsh realization that I wasn't going to play my position. I didn't want to go to college if I couldn't play quarterback." Growing up, he had a few family members that had joined the Army. " A guidance counselor in high school referred me over to Army recruiter. I went down, did well on the test, and decided to enlist."

"I was fortunate enough that throughout my entire career, I found favor with people and leaders that kind of saw potential in me." Lindsey trusted them in guiding his path, where he was told who to hang with and who not to hang with, what courses to take, and what type of military and civilian education to pursue. "I put my career completely in the hands of leaders. It wasn't until much later, maybe around the seventeen- or eighteen-year mark, that I started to take control of my future. Up until that point, I had leaders that I trusted."

As the top senior enlisted positions became increasingly competitive, Lindsey knew that based where he ranked with my peers that he had an opportunity. "I began to be a little more deliberate in what I was doing. I got heavily involved in completing my civilian education going, earned three college degrees and encouraged hundreds of my soldiers to do the same." He soon earned the rank of Command Sergeant Major.

"I proudly served for 31 years. Honestly, I never expected it to go that long". At the 20-year mark, Lindsey looked ahead. With three children heading to college at the same time, he decided the Army would continue to provide the stability he and his family wanted. During that time, his family continued to live in the DC area while Lindsey rotated from base to base. "Over time, my responsibilities changed, but my passion for recruiting remained the same."

## THE TRANSITION

Approaching 31 years, Lindsey was on a list to become a nominative Sergeant Major. "I was going through the interview process to go and work at the General Officer level as their senior list advisor. At the time, my wife had just finished her second bout with breast cancer which was very nasty." Wanting to remove emotion from the decision, he sought divine intervention on whether to stay or go and said a prayer on the ride home from work one day.

"A few minutes after saying the prayer my phone rang. It was a good friend of mine that had worked with me some nine years earlier and he asked me what I was doing." Lindsey said, "I'm contemplating whether to stay in or get out." His friend told him of a job that had opened up at his company and asked for a resume. He told Lindsey that they wanted to do more with transitioning veterans and felt it would be a fit. "It was powerful. It was so powerful."

Moving to the civilian world was a bit of a stretch, but Lindsey trusted his friend. "He felt I would fit in the culture and saw something in me knowing it was a match. What I didn't expect was the collaborative nature of the business. It was collaborative to the point where it slowed down movement decisions. I had to get a little use to that."

Lindsey worked at the company headquarters in the small business credit card division. "It was within the targeting strategy of the company and how it positions cards out into the market. About a month in it all made sense. I remembered how Army recruiting command targeted its recruits and how it marketed to them, and it was the same concepts and principles. Once I understood that, I got into the driver's seat with my career."

He quickly moved through the ranks, soon becoming a Market Leader. "I led clusters of banks from five to 25 banks in a market, applying leadership and oversight to those markets was my new goal in the company."

## LESSONS LEARNED

"People talk about this network thing and how important it is or how beneficial it is. Not a lot of veterans understand this. The ability to reach into an organization through someone that you know and trust, someone that can do the bidding for you, someone that can speak for you, someone that could tell a hiring manager something about you that's not written on a resume. It's so valuable!"

## WHAT'S NEXT

Now the SVP of Global Military Affairs at Bank of America, Lindsey maintains the company's military relationships globally. "It includes all of the governmental agencies and the nonprofit partnerships that we have. Internally I look at everything that touches a veteran here at the company, from how we meet and recruit them, to how we onboard and assimilate them. I also look at the attrition and performance of our veterans, leveraging that information to influence policy and decision regarding how we interact with veterans and military families within the company."

"After the passing of my wife, I made the decision to stay in Savannah, Georgia." Growing up, sports made a difference in his life. Knowing that sports would attract kids to athletes and their heroes, he decided to bring a sports franchise to Savannah. The goal was to leverage the pro athletes into the community with different youth groups and organizations to try and influence behavior through the example of the players. At halftime of a basketball game, we swore in five kids who took the oath of enlistment in front of nearly 400 veterans that were in the audience. it was just a way of referencing the past and then acknowledging this future force that's going to be served."

"That is the vision of the Savannah Hurricane basketball team. We make a way for them to come see us play basketball and then we make our players available so those kids can touch them. We're off and running with many community partners including the YMCA, the National Guard Youth Challenge Program, and the Army Recruiting Command. Lindsey wants the team to be in a legacy." He also hopes to one day write some books documenting his journey.

## THE MILITARY EFFECT

"Going into corporate America, I had to get accustomed to the dress there. The army had my clothes picked out for me for the most part. And then business acumen. There's an opportunity for all veterans in transition to grasp the required language lexicon of where they're going next. Our skills are often masked in military specific jargon. It takes a bit of unpacking and un-studying what exactly it is that we did while in, and how that translates over to where we're going next. But once you're able to do that, speed kicks in right away and you're able to really move fast."

# 27

## MARK ZINNO, ARMY

linkedin.com/in/mark-zinno-2960bb88
**Hometown:** *Long Island, New York*
**Currently Resides:** *Atlanta, Georgia*

## WHY I SERVED

Growing up, Mark had grand aspirations to play professional sports. "Looking at college, everywhere I wanted to go was too pricey." His stepfather, a Vietnam veteran, suggested he go after an ROTC scholarship. "I wasn't really interested in service but knew they would pay for school."

Soon after enrolling he secured a three-year Army ROTC scholarship. Said Mark, "I always thought I would do four years and get out, but then 9/11 happened. I never expected to stay for almost 25 years. For me it was a means to an end and a way to pay for college."

While in service, the Clinton administration created a combat reform initiative. It sent incentives to the officers to the guard to finish their careers. "It was a quiet time, and we weren't at war. Our forces were being downsized to pre-WWII levels." Mark was one of those selected, being sent off active duty three months before 9/11.

"After that had happened, it kind of changed the view for me. That was my city. There were kids I grew up with and friends in those buildings. It was kind of personal." A couple of years later, Mark ended up on his first deployment. "It took me some time to buy in and to get my head on straight, and even longer to really understand what I was a part of."

## THE TRANSITION

Getting sent off active duty, Mark will never forget the battalion commander looked him dead in the eyes and said, "You sure you want to do this? Because you're really good at this, and I'm not sure you should really walk away from it just yet."

"It survived my college years, my post college years, and my marriage. It's helped me raise my kids. It's the one relationship that's never quit on me. So why should I quit on it? I mean, in reality, I've spent more of my life in uniform than I have out of it. I got in uniform at 21, 46 now. You do the math. I've been in uniform longer than not."

"Being in the Guard gives me the best of both worlds because I still love putting the uniform on and I still love giving back." Mark has been offered deployments over the past year or two and turned them down. "When you spend time in the Guard or the Reserves and you're still doing the civilian life and everything else, it's a delicate balance at the time. I've been fortunate enough to work for employers who have been very understanding. It allowed me the bandwidth to get called up for hurricanes and civil disturbance and COVID response for months at a time where it wasn't an issue."

After leaving active duty and going into the Guard, Mark spent a few years working in random civilian jobs. "They were very low paying jobs at small radio stations. I climbed up the mountain doing news and traffic for a news station at one point."

"The first job I got was a play-by-play job for my alma mater, doing college basketball before I deployed. I'd actually done some public address announcing for them at the basketball games."

He continues, "The radio career was something I always wanted to do. I just wanted to be around sports. The two worlds merged together for me. I wanted to be in sports broadcasting. It's what I went to college for. I had to put it on hold because of active duty and the military and everything else."

Mark started to make many connections and landed a job at WNAV, a small local news station in Annapolis, Maryland. "Eventually I got a sports anchor job and before you knew it, I was hosting the show."

## LESSONS LEARNED

Without empathy, conversations are just transactional.

## WHAT'S NEXT

Mark's podcast, The Hazard Ground - Tales of Combat and Survival continues to grow. "We discuss the physical effects of combat and everything else going on. Our focus is around mental health, PTSD prevention, and transition to the civilian world." Gaining worldwide attention from its listeners, the show will soon be celebrating its 7th year. Says Mark, "It's an incredible platform. I've received letters from as far away as Australia and England. We have been fortunate to share hundreds of stories from our guests."

"I love what I do. I never get out of bed in the morning stressed going to work. My kids will hear my stuff and see my stuff. They told me a week ago that they Googled me. I'm like, you're eight years old. How do you know what Google is? Stop googling, dad." He adds, "Even when I'm doing ESPN radio, their mother will put it on for them just for a little bit just to hear me and let them know that daddy is on the radio, and they get to tell their friends about it."

Still part of the Reserves, Mark reflects, "I'm a different leader now as a Colonel than I ever was before. And I keep working on that craft and honing it and refining it and everything else. The military made me a great leader, but I made myself a better leader by embracing that whole ideology as something that was important. I want to leave a legacy with people."

## THE MILITARY EFFECT

"I would tell this to anybody who's still in the service that, you know, much like you would plan for a mission ahead of time or you would train for mission at a time, train for your exit practice for your exit. Figure out where your next platoon is, your next team, your next company, whatever it may be. That's, that's a hard part of transition for a lot of us."

# 28

## MARLENE ANDERSCH, AIR FORCE

linkedin.com/in/mandersch
**Hometown:** *Seattle, Washington*
**Currently Resides:** *Raleigh, North Carolina*

## WHY I SERVED

Marlie wanted to see the world! After high school, her plan was to take a year off and travel before she started college. "My friend and I went to the mall where he enlisted in the Army." As she waited on a bench outside of the Army office, a recruiter from the Air Force walked up and asked if she had any plans after high school. "I was immediately interested, because I could defer my enlistment, travel before basic training, and the Air Force would pay for my college."

Already receiving several college scholarship offers, her decision to join the military surprised many. "Why you? You are going to join the Air Force and be like Private Benjamin (a movie about a privileged woman who joined the military thinking it would be an easy vacation)." It was the best thing she could have done. "Serving our country was an amazing experience that helped nurture and shape my mentality. Despite gender, race, religion, and family cultures, the military taught us the importance of camaraderie, discipline, respect for authority and how to unite for the mission."

After tech school, the first Gulf War had started and Marlie was sent overseas to Clark Air Base in the Philippines. As soon as she arrived, there was an assassination of two Airman. Shortly after a catastrophic 7.7 magnitude earthquake, Marlie was part of the team that helped provide rescue operations. Her resilience was then really tested when the Mt Pinatubo volcano erupted. "Our unit was tasked with evacuating over 10,000 civilians from Clark Air Base to Subic Bay Naval Station, over 60 miles away. I remember many families had very little time to gather their belongings, while we watched a mushroom cloud of volcanic ash that was ready to rain down on us." Upon returning to Clark, Marlie discovered there was over a foot of ash covering the base and limited resources for food, transportation, and housing. After helping to close down the base, she was then stationed at Seymour Johnson Air Force Base in North Carolina.

## THE TRANSITION

Entering right into the work force after separating from the Air Force, Marlie's transition was a smooth one. She balanced a hefty schedule with a full-time job at IBM, school at night, and working at the hospital on the weekends. Her goal was to be a surgeon, but volunteer work at the hospital allowed her to see that the job and environment were not what she expected. "The reason I wanted to be a doctor, is because I wanted to help people. But my experience within the health sector was not a positive one." She changed her career choice and made the decision to pursue another passion in technology.

With each passing day in the office, Marlie knew her focus had shifted from medicine to data. "We had just started using green screen computers as we transitioned from the typewriter. With my work performance, my boss knew I had a career at IBM." This fueled Marlie's competitive spirit, and she went full force into the technology sector.

After a few years, Marlie continued her path in the industry. She spent time working at a variety of tech companies in roles which included everything from coding, business development and alliances. The larger the company, the bigger the title, and that came with challenges. "Over time, I was getting tired of the internal politics and processes required to do good business and provide great services to our clients." Marlie knew it was time to start her own company. "I always knew I could do it, and the time was right!"

Marlie left her full-time job a few months later and rockITdata was launched. It was one of the worst times anyone could have started a company, as the Pandemic struck. "We bootstrapped it at the beginning, and it wasn't easy. We struggled with people, systems, processes, funding, operations like HR and finance. There had been several times where I debated going back to corporate life with a salary and benefits." Shortly after getting rockITdata off the ground, she was introduced to her now business partner. During his career, he built a company and sold it to another large consulting firm. Years later when she asked him "why get back into business?" He said, "There's only so much hunting and fishing you can do...let's keep rockITdata going and build an amazing business."

Through her network, Marlie was introduced to another company and rockITdata started providing Salesforce development services. While servicing clients, it was uncovered that rockITdata had owner designations that large companies and the federal government deemed valuable. These larger companies all have supplier diversity goals that encouraged them to work with companies like rockITdata. "I didn't know that being a woman, minority and veteran owned company gave us opportunities to compete with larger established IT consulting firms."

rockITdata was growing and at almost 350% year over year, as its technology services were widely needed even with the onset of COVID. "We started using AI/ML models before it was cool and with our supplier diversity opportunities, we took off!"

## LESSONS LEARNED

Change your mindset to change your outcomes.

## WHAT'S NEXT

rockITdata has grown to almost 200 employees and contractors, hyper focused on providing exceptional services to our customers. "We have evolved into a company that provides professional services, with a focus on data analytics, AI/ML in healthcare life sciences, state, local, education and the federal government. As we continue to grow, we stand by our guiding principles that enable the culture we desire. rockITdata wins when we hire rockstars that abide by our values, they have entrepreneurial spirit, integrity, and grit. A lot of our employees are from the veteran community, which inspires our culture. We march in the direction of mission with purpose."

Her firm continues to expand with employees and contractors in forty states and two countries. Says Marlie, "rockITdata will continue to focus on growth and we are always looking for new opportunities." The firm is busy spinning up more service options to clients in the health care and regulated industry sectors.

## THE MILITARY EFFECT

"Many veterans are risk adverse. We spent years serving to protect our country. We understand respect for authority and process. When you get out, it can be a hard transition. Surround yourself with people that want to help and support you. There are so many opportunities and programs that are focused on helping the veteran. The civilian world and corporate America are a different world. Trust in yourself and believe in you."

# 29

## MATTHEW GRIFFIN, ARMY

**Hometown:** *Eldridge, Iowa*
**Currently Resides:** *Volcano, Hawaii*

### WHY I SERVED

Matthew is fourth generation military. He still has the military records and horseback riding certificates from his great grandfather who fought in WWI. "Grandpa Eddie left the US at the age of 17, got on a boat and sailed to England. He became a tail gunner in an A-20 havoc, which was a really rare British war plane. They were the guys going after the ball bearing factories. He got shot down on his 52nd mission over France. And I still have his purple heart."

"Grandpa Melstrom, William, was a cartographer for the Navy in the Pacific. He was one of the guys that helped find the Cuban missiles." Matthew didn't find out any of the stories till he was much older, and they had passed away. "I always wondered why we were around his house in Northern Virginia there were guns stashed everywhere."

A West Point graduate in 1973, Matthew's father just barely missed the Vietnam War. "I think he had a chip on his shoulder about that. He went on to serve 20 years as an armor officer." His father went back to West Point as an instructor in the early 80's. "When we were there, we used to have cadets over to the house and I would see how my parents respected these young cadets. I was only three then, and that stuck with me."

As graduation from high school approached, Matthew knew it was his turn. The family didn't have lots of money so he would have to get a job, a scholarship or join the military. "I did all three and went to West Point. I still remember sitting in the officer's basic course when the towers fell on 9/11."

He went to become a Ranger Fire Support Officer. "I could call anything out of the sky that I wanted at any point in time. I worked with tremendous leaders."

### THE TRANSITION

"I was living a life of danger and didn't think I'd make it to my 30th birthday." Matthew was mapping out his future, and none of the roles he would graduate into seemed very appealing. "Seeing the job opportunities ahead, I knew they would take me away from the family more." It became even more apparent as his first daughter, Estella, was born while Matthew was standing on the hood of a Humvee in Afghanistan. He got out in 2006.

The Wounded Warrior project had just started. Like many nonprofits, one of its focus areas is to help veterans get employed. "I went to this job fair and met a former Marine captain and he worked for this large homebuilder called Centex Homes. He says, 'Come work for me, I'll teach you a trade. I'll teach you a skill. You can go anywhere and do this. He focused on bringing in junior military officers and junior NCOs to run his job sites because he knew veterans could get the job done."

In 2008, after losing his job as a homebuilder the year before, Matthew went to work for Remote Medical International. "They were the experts at providing medical services in clinics and advanced gear for the gas mineral and oil industries operating all over the earth on these remote sites and putting in clinics." He continues, "While in these regions. I would stay above a grocery store or a coffee shop or whatever. And I would hire the owner's brother as my driver and fixer to get me around to places. And it was the same thing everywhere."

One day Matthew walked into a combat boot factory in Kabul, Afghanistan. "Having served there, I had a very negative mindset. But the experience turned out to be positive. I saw what our government said we were going to do. Now I had one thing that I could point to that all that time and sacrifice was worth it. " He was truly inspired. "While visiting a local factory I asked the manager what they were going to make when the war ended. And he said, "Nothing. All these people are going to be out of work. Nobody's going to want to buy anything from Afghanistan."

Matthew went from inspiration to fury in probably two to three breaths. "In that moment of frustration and anger I looked down on this table and I saw this combat boot sole with a flip-flop thong punch through it.". Combat Flip Flops was born. "We are combat flip flops as a person. It's not just a piece of footwear. It's somebody who believes that, hey, we can do things better. We even trademarked the phrase, 'Be a better human.'" The factory in Kabul was launched.

"After multiple failures, we found out that it was logistically and financially impossible to make footwear in Afghanistan. We shifted our production to Bogota, Columbia, and in Afghanistan started making textiles. Then we went to Laos and started making jewelry from landmines like over from the Vietnam War."

## LESSONS LEARNED

Fail Cheap. Learn fast.

# WHAT'S NEXT

"We are looking for as much PR as we can get. I will talk about our mission to help others in war zones as often as somebody wants to listen to me talk about it." Matthew is now a professional public speaker, giving presentations to companies like American Express & Amazon. He says, "If you need somebody to come and speak at an event, you know, that's how I pay for my lifestyle."

You don't make a lot of money-making flip flops in war zones. But I gotta tell you what, I'm happy and enjoy what I do. I enjoy the people that I work with. My team is amazing." Combat Flip Flops used its profits recently to put over one thousand girls to school in Afghanistan.

Recently remarried, Matthew and his wife bought a small ranch in Hawaii and moved there. "I think mentorship is a thing that we all need to take seriously. When I coach young veteran entrepreneurs on it, I have a line, 'fail cheap and learn fast'. If you're gonna push forward on something don't throw the whole bank on it, try to minimize your risk. It's all about risk mitigation but if you try something and fail at least it didn't cost you four or five six figures. Learn from it, and how can you approach it again."

# THE MILITARY EFFECT

"I think that one of the main problems veterans have, is coming from a community of problem solvers where a lot was on the line, and then going into a traditional workplace environment where there's not a loss of life on the line and problems are just problems that are solvable. We are hardworking team players and problem solvers that are willing to contribute to whoever gives us an opportunity to do better. We need to learn how to be a good subordinate in a corporate environment."

# 30

## MEAGHAN MOBBS, ARMY

linkedin.com/in/meaghan-mobbs-phd-51b50b156
**Hometown:** *Ft Myer, Virginia*
**Currently Resides:** *Vienna, Virginia*

## WHY I SERVED

Meaghan grew up in a home of paratroopers. Her mom was one of the first group of women admitted to Airborne School, her father had a 36-year career, and her brother followed in her footsteps. "It was the family business". She was surrounded by stories and lived on military bases her whole life. "Honestly, I never considered it as a career. When I was in kindergarten, I wanted to be an Army wife because I saw how hard my mom worked as one."

In high school during sophomore year, 9/11 happened. Her father was at the Pentagon that day.

"Like many that day, it completely changed the trajectory of my life. I wanted to enlist as soon as I graduated and become a combat medic(68 Whiskey)". Going into college Meaghan was encouraged to enter ROTC, as both of her parents had, and they also told her to look at the United States Military Academy - West Point.

During an overnight cadet candidate visit at West Point she was walking with a cadet. "It was freezing out, and we put our hands in pockets to keep them warm. The cadet got yelled at." Meaghan thought to herself that she would never accept that. "The next summer I went back for summer camp and fell in love. This is where I wanted to be."

Always working hard, Meaghan graduated at the top of her class. She was given her first choice of branch and went to Fort Bragg. "I was commissioned as a Quartermaster officer. Being a paratrooper, I wanted to jump." This focus continued in the officer basic course where she was the honor graduate. Meaghan was given the opportunity to attend rigger school and learned how to pack and repair parachutes. "I became the parachute pack platoon leader for the 82nd Airborne Division."

On her cherry jump(first jump) in division at Fort Bragg, both parents came down to watch. "They were so excited to see their daughter jump on the drop zones they jumped into." The Sicily Drop is very famous there, allowing mass drops of paratroopers. Sitting in the bleachers with their binoculars, they waited for Meaghan as she was the platoon leader and expected to jump first. "I managed to find the one tree on Sicily Drop Zone and landed on top of it, bear hugging the tree."

Being too high, she couldn't get down without help.

## THE TRANSITION

During her tour in Afghanistan, Meaghan was introduced to her first mentor who was one of the first psychologists for Delta (the Tier 1 Special Operators), he helped design the selection assessment course, and tried to begin to understand the psychology of warfighting. Soon he posed a question. "You are good with logistics, and great with people. Have you ever thought about going back to school and doing work in psychology?" Meaghan had not.

After commanding an aerial delivery detachment in Afghanistan, she got out in 2013. "I was still on active duty the last few months and my husband was deployed. So having two young daughters I moved in with my parents and went to school at night to get my masters."

With a new direction, she transitioned out and became a Tillman scholar, getting her master's degree in forensic and Operational Psychology. Her studies were under Jerry Post, one of the first psychiatrists for the Central Intelligence Agency. It was an important move and helped her to get a doctorate at Columbia.

At Columbia, Meaghan had the distinct pleasure of treating former special operators who were in the General Studies program. Established post World War II, it was established as a way to ensure that GIs had the opportunity to access an Ivy League education and recruits heavily from the special operations community.

"I built a glide path for myself. Get to the end state. These are the things I have to do".

Meaghan has always been interested in the extremes of human behavior and understanding that side of things. "The world is dangerous. There is always a necessity of assessing and selecting people capable of defending our nation. I wanted to be a part of that and whatever it took to increase the lethality of our armed forces, especially on the human side." She goes on to say, "Warfare is still inherently a human endeavor, even with all the AI and drones."

## LESSONS LEARNED

Amateurs discuss tactics. Experts discuss logistics.

## WHAT'S NEXT

Currently the president of the R.T. Weatherman Foundation, Meaghan is also committed to a number of other initiatives. "I'm on the Boards of Global Response Medicine, and the Virginia Military Institute." She also dedicates time as a Senior Fellow with the Independent Women's Forum.

Under The Weatherman Foundation, Meaghan says, "The best work we are doing is coming out of the veteran vertical, specifically focused on the evacuation of wounded Americans and repatriation of Americans killed in action in Ukraine."

"I have always had a hard time saying no to things and will continue to expand my schedule to fit it in. Especially if it interests me." Meaghan tries to be intentional about the things she does, always investing time in meeting with others face-to-face. "Being successful comes with your ability to harness people and reach outcomes."

She adds, "Half of my organizations are veterans. When possible, I recruit them. Especially in the humanitarian space. There is a deep reluctance to engage with former military. I think there is a belief that we are incapable, or maybe less apt to be compassionate humanitarians."

## THE MILITARY EFFECT.

"There is no greater alumni group than being a military veteran. Everybody I know in life is either a veteran themselves or one degree removed. It's only because the military invested in me. Without this network I would never be as successful as I am now."

# 31

## MICAH NIEBAUER, ARMY

linkedin.com/in/micahniebauer
**Hometown:** *Superior, Wisconsin*
**Currently Resides:** *Southern Pines, North Carolina*

### WHY I SERVED

Growing up in Wisconsin, Micah had two goals: to play baseball and be in the army. He was surrounded by the military. "We had a neighbor whose grandfather was a B-2 Bomber pilot in WW2. And my uncle was a Command Star Major in the Army who served in Vietnam and went on to work for JAG." One of the first letters he ever wrote was asking his uncle for some military stuff. "He sent me many things, including some clothes that I wore everywhere."

With college on the horizon, it was time to figure out how to pay for it. "I went to school in Chicago and knew I wanted to be in the army, so I joined ROTC." Micah wasn't able to get a scholarship that first year and made the most of it by joining crew and becoming the class president. But as a sophomore he secured one for the remaining three years.

"I always thought I would work in government, so I took classes in international relations and interned in DC." Micah also knew that his time in the military would help him to better understand foreign policy, which he was fascinated by. And then 9/11 happened. "I entered the military, became an infantry officer in the 82nd Airborne, and did two deployments to Afghanistan and one to Iraq."

### THE TRANSITION

"Wars were changing, and so was my job. There were no more opportunities to lead in combat." The culture was changing for Micah, and he wasn't sure he could influence change anymore. Says Micah, "By going into Special Forces, it gave me a longer period of time to serve But, I knew my time had come to move on."

The idea of entrepreneurship was always there for Micah. He was aware of the American Dream. Even though it wasn't a focus while serving, Micah would often attend local dinners & banquets with his wife, who is an attorney. "At one fundraiser I met an angel investor. At the time, I had no idea what that even meant." The gentlemen went on to tell him about a brewery he was invested in called Lonerider Brewery. It sparked an idea!

Arriving home, Micah called one of his team members, and they decided to leave the military and start a brewery. "We didn't know where to start, even though I was basically a strategic planner in the military." They sat down with SCORE to learn how to write a business plan, but it didn't provide the guidance they sought. Says Micah, "It wasn't really helpful, so we relied on our background. Entrepreneurship has become our new foxhole. It's a fascinating way to live your life."

Southern Pines Brewing was the first to enter the local market, recently celebrating their 9ᵗʰ anniversary. "So many people didn't know what craft beer was. Even the distributors had to be taught about it." Micah and his partner were proud to be veterans but didn't want customers simply because they served. They struggled with how to integrate the brand into their business model. "We downplayed our service and reached out to the entire community. But it didn't matter, as we soon became known as veteran entrepreneurs." Because of this status, a major retail chain promoted the brand in their stores and offered discounts to customers.

## LESSONS LEARNED

Reacting to your mistakes quickly will produce the best outcomes.

## WHAT'S NEXT

Exciting plans are in the works for Southern Pines Brewing, as they expand to Carthage and Fayetteville, NC. "Our expansion will include adding food for the first time. We were fortunate to bring on a former military spouse who was a very successful chef." Micah also has his eye on additional states (they are also in South Carolina), as well as offering new products.

"I have truly enjoyed the progression of my business journey. It's our goal to create and foster community by continuously reimagining the craft beverage and hospitality experience." Next up is a cocktail brand and bottled spirits. They also hope to offer some non-alcoholic brands. With a thirst for knowledge, he recently enrolled in a management program at Harvard Business School. Says Micah, "I would love to create a multi-generational company. It's fun to think about the children entering our business."

## THE MILITARY EFFECT

"The military does not teach you about business, and it's a steep learning curve coming out." His advice? Become a lifelong learner or you will be left behind. "It's the same in the business world as it is in the military. When you want to lead, there are no shortcuts."

# 32

## MICHELLE "MACE" CURRAN, AIR FORCE

linkedin.com/in/macecurran
**Hometown:** *Medford, Wisconsin*
**Currently Resides:** *Las Vegas, Nevada*

## WHY I SERVED

Growing up in a small town in Wisconsin, Michelle always wanted to go to college and explore the world. "I wanted to be an FBI agent and studied criminal justice." Her goal was to just be a normal college student. However, to help pay for college, she joined ROTC, and became aware of cool things going on in the Air Force. In her sophomore year, everything changed.

Says Michelle, "My only connection to the military was from my grandfather who fought in World War II. "I didn't really grow up in a military or aviation family. It wasn't until a base visit to Tyndall Air Force Base that I became seriously interested in flying." Seeing two F-15 jets up close for the first time taking off during sunset she was hooked. "Holy crap, how do I do that? It was life changing and gave me goosebumps." Being adventurous and wanting to see the world, she put her name in the hat to compete for a pilot spot....and got one. From that moment on she had one goal: To become a fighter pilot.

Making this happen was not easy, and Michelle was the only woman in her class of 25 during undergraduate Pilot Training. "I didn't think about gender being a factor, but it was soon highlighted." Pilot training was a lot of work, and often felt like drinking from a firehouse. Classes had only been receiving one or two fighter pilot slots, so Michelle knew the odds were against her. Her efforts left to snagging one of the two spots her class received and she was sent to learn to fly the F-16.

"I was awarded a fighter slot. Some said because it checked the diversity box, but I earned it." Once she reached her first fighter squadron, Michelle had to learn the tactics and culture. Constantly under the microscope, Michelle became a litmus test for what would be accepted in her unit. It was a stressful job, and much more complicated than just simple flying. She had to become an expert in tactics, the system of the aircraft, and how the battlespace works. "It was often overwhelming."

Getting into The Thunderbirds happened thanks to the intersection of hard work and opportunity. Perhaps a bit of luck was involved as well. "I only found out that the Thunderbirds were accepting applications through an email. The team had sent out several announcements and this was the final one sent (and the first one Michelle read)." Having another assignment already teed up, she almost passed on it. "My mentor encouraged me to apply and said I would be a great Thunderbird." Offering his assistance, the two scrambled to submit the needed information. It was a tremendous workload, but the efforts paid off.

In its history, The Thunderbirds have had about 300 pilots. Michelle was the 4th female ever in the demonstration. "I knew it would be fun & challenging and was drawn to the mission. I was so excited to inspire others just by doing my job." For three years, she spent 240 days on the road per year, and flew more than 1000 hours. Once, a few years before applying to the Thunderbirds while based in Japan, she had a short conversation with a Japanese woman. "There were no fighter pilots in their air force, and she wanted to be the first one. She told me It was my flying that fueled her goal and that interaction helped fuel mine."

# THE TRANSITION

After leaving the Thunderbirds, Michelle's visibility was high. "I was booked for speaking appearances, offered obscure consulting opportunities, and approached to be the face of some brands." She had to learn what to say no to, and over time found her groove.

New opportunities came primarily from LinkedIn and Instagram in the form of speaking engagements. "I got great advice early on to become very active online." Michelle posted almost every day. The message was authentic and consistent, giving credibility to her story. "In less than a year and a half I gained 20,000 followers on LinkedIn, a platform I hadn't been active on before."

Being an entrepreneur has not been an easy transition, but Michelle gets her motivation from her audience. "I once gave a presentation for a group of construction contractors. It was primarily men, and kind of intimidating. My talk was on being bold, taking calculated risks, and reframing our inner critic. At the end, a big man approached me. He said he had been waiting to find something life changing he could implement from this conference, and I had just given him that."

Now Michelle's speaking career has taken off. Literally! "My business has grown from personal introductions, people reaching out to me through social media, and the speaking gigs themselves." With business growing quickly, she started to hire key employees. One was the person who had given her advice on writing on LinkedIn. "He played the long game," Michelle said. "I did not hesitate to hire him to manage my content when it became too much to stay on top of."

Last summer, Michelle did an event in Brazil for John Deer Latin America. Her audience was over 3,000 people. "The reception from all of these heavy hitters has been awesome. And I'm very easy to work with." She's been surprised by some questions from the event coordinators. "I have been asked if I want a certain kind of water in my hotel room. Or do you need blue M&Ms? I was like, people ask for this stuff. I just came off of Active Duty for 13 years. I'm just happy to be staying at a Marriott."

## LESSONS LEARNED

Find others to be your wingman

## WHAT'S NEXT

Michelle loves the flexibility of being an entrepreneur and continues to move forward. With creative control to say yes or no, the focus is on what works best for her lifestyle and keeps her excited. In the year ahead she is expecting to book 40 keynotes. "I'm hitting big stages now and it's an honor."

"So many great opportunities are being put in front of me." The list continues to grow, and she is excited for all of them. "I had been approached by a network to consult on a movie about the Thunderbirds. Others want to do documentaries to tell the stories of female pilots. The market is so strong right now because of characters like Captain Marvel and Phoenix from the new Top Gun movie." She goes on to say, "I love to see mainstream media sharing these stories because that is how it becomes normalized for the next generation."

With so much to tell, Michelle also released a best-selling children's book last year. It's about a little girl who wants to be a fighter pilot and is the first in a three-book series. She is also working on her first personal development book for adults.

## THE MILITARY EFFECT

One of Michelle's favorite stories is of a follower that reached out via direct message. "She had just graduated college via Air Force ROTC, following a similar path to mine. Her goals were the same, and she wanted to be a fighter pilot." Almost two years passed with no updates. "One day I got a message that she had just found out she was going to fly the F-16. It was amazing news!". To this day, Michelle has yet to meet her but is happy to know the advice and encouragement she shared might have helped his aspiring pilot.

# 33

## MIKE SARRAILLE, NAVY

linkedin.com/in/michaelsarraille
**Hometown:** *Atherton, California*
**Currently Resides:** *Austin, Texas*

## WHY I SERVED

Mike didn't come from a traditional military family. He was an average teenager, choosing fun and adventure over academics. However, Mike knew that he wanted to challenge himself, he just didn't know which path to take.

"When I was about eight or nine, we were on a highway in California behind a five-ton truck with soldiers in it. My dad said they were Green Berets." He remembers waving to them, and they were waving back. "Slowly the military started to grab ahold of me. in the large part it was due to Hollywood." This was a big factor in pushing Mike towards the military and Special Forces.

A student at the University of Colorado, he didn't last long with the NROTC. But, as fate would have it, Mike was introduced to Force Recon Marine. "Along the way I had met many rude officers, or senior midshipmen, who leaned on their positional authority. But this guy was humbly confident, kind, respectful and empathetic. He was different from all the rest." He helped him enlist. "He knew I just needed a purpose, discipline and a tribe."

That's what got Michael into the military. "It was a Marine Recon contract. I made it and became a Recon Marine and scout sniper within my first year in the Marine Corps." For Mike, the Marine Corps laid the foundation for him to be successful, not only in the SEALs but in the private sector. "Without them, I would not be the man I am today".

The Marine Corps eventually sent Mike back to college to finish his degree and commission as an officer, but he made a last-minute decision to commission in the Navy and try out for the SEAL teams. He made it and served his remaining career as a SEAL officer.

## THE TRANSITION

After 10 combat deployments, Mike was ready for a change. "I just lost steam. I lost a sense of purpose in the war, which was coming to a close. It was the hardest decision I ever had to make to leave my tribe. Because my

DNA is, is team is being part of tribe." As part of the SEAL teams, he had a strong support mechanism. "My leaders cared about me, knew I needed a recharge and wanted to get back near my family in Texas."

Coming home, Mike had to become a new person. "What helped me tremendously was sitting down with good friends and talking through things. It was important to talk through things, and not just let them fester inside me." Soon, he got a tour of the University of Texas and became an instructor at the Naval ROTC. While there he enrolled for his MBA.

Not long after, The Vetted Foundation was launched with the help of mentors Admiral McRaven, Admiral Bobby Inman & General Tony Cucolo. "I worked with Wharton, The McCombs Business School and the Mays Business School at Texas A&M to develop a mini-MBA program for veterans coming out." It featured a pilot class, which was Mike's foray into raising money. "I wasn't skilled at this, but we were very successful. Even the Huffington Post praised it as having the way to revolutionize how veterans exit the military."

From all the data accumulated in the program, the Vetted Foundation initiated a research project to identify the systemic challenges facing veterans. "One of the things that we found is that there's a lack of financial acumen. So, this one-month program and this mini-MBA, which also had transition services and career services, taught business acumen. It was highly successful." After a short stint overseeing all veteran services for the Texas A&M system, Mike found his calling. "It was my foray into leadership development. Something I'm passionate about."

## LESSONS LEARNED

"I always liked being part of a good team. I was never the strongest soldier, never the fastest, never the brightest. But man, I was part of some amazing teams. no matter what you threw at us with unwavering optimism, we would find a path to success."

## WHAT'S NEXT

"I want to write a book on leadership for the next generation." All his efforts focus on positive impact, and messages that resonate. Mike has started several companies and wrote his first book The *Talent War: How Special Operations and Great Organizations Win on Talent*. But he didn't stop there. He wrote his second book, *The Everyday Warrior,* focused on self-help, or as Mike refers to it, self-leadership. His efforts are all tied together, and now a new endeavor called Legacy Expeditions has started. "I'm going where life is taking me. It's not what I had envisioned but I'm enjoying it."

The Founder of Legacy Expeditions, Mike's mission is to bring world record-setting attempts and expeditions to life while upholding the memories and legacies of U.S. and Allied troops lost during the Global War on Terrorism.

Legacy Expeditions is a boutique extreme adventure and leadership development firm and led by retired Tier One Operators and Special Operations soldiers, Legacy Expeditions plans, coordinates, and executes exclusive extreme adventures designed to promote personal growth by pushing participants to their mental and physical limits, what is often referred to as experiential leadership development.

On his podcast, The Men's Journal Everyday Warrior, Mike gets to share stories of others in service. "I am in awe of the men and women I served. I've said it, but I just enjoy this storytelling component because its oral history passed down." He hopes that each show provides at least one key takeaway that can be implemented in their lives.

He's also working on ways to tell their stories of fallen soldiers through those that served with them. " How many documentaries have you watched in your tears at the end? You're like, damn, I need to do more". Mike works hard to share more and loves this self-discovery. "I'm still going through that process. Doing this is slowly becoming a major passion. It's just hard to monetize it. And I'm working through that right now."

## THE MILITARY EFFECT

"In my opinion, there needs to be a military culture exclusion or protection act from our civilian leaders trying to transform the military culture into progressive policies that the civilian world has. The military culture is unique. We put an emphasis on things like conformity, standards, and team over individual. The civilian sector is built differently. putting a precedence on individuality, and you won't find that same homecoming and belonging in the private sector."

# 34

## MISTY COOK, MARINES

linkedin.com/in/mistycook
**Hometown:** *Bridge City, Texas*
**Currently Resides:** *Washington, D.C.*

## WHY I SERVED

Married at 18 to a hometown guy, who was already a Marine, Misty followed him to his first station in Hawaii. "About six months into our marriage, I had a daily routine of going to college during the day, then spending my nights spit-shining boots and pressing his uniforms. I saw this camaraderie that I had as an athlete in high school and wanted that feeling again." Misty knew she wanted to join the Marines and soon enlisted.

"I ended up being an aviation maintenance administrator, staying there for about four years." Then her husband applied for an officer program and the following year Misty followed suit. "I applied to what we call MECEP, which is the Marine Enlisted Commissioning Education Program. The Marine Corps will allow you to come out of the Operating Forces and send you to college, you commission and then you owe them years on the back end. I attended The Citadel, The Military College of South Carolina and got my degree in Criminal Justice. I went back a few years later and earned a Master's in Pre-Law."

Earning her commission, Misty knew deep down that she belonged here. "I found my purpose and loved leading Marines. At The Basic School (TBS), Marines are able to list their military occupational specialty (MOS) preferences for assignments, but nothing's guaranteed. For me, I knew I wanted to be an Adjutant—administrative role, which means it is not on the top of many lists, but it's so much more than just paperwork. You're the heartbeat of the unit (at least I felt I was), handling everything from accountability to legal matters and casualty reports. And when you're out there deployed as an Adjutant, that's when your attention to detail and compassion truly come to the forefront. It's in those moments that you realize the impact you're making."

"I occupied the office through which every piece of paperwork from the company had to pass before reaching the Battalion for approval. Every document crossed my desk, placing me in a pivotal role to provide unwavering support to our Marines in every conceivable manner." Whether it was sorting out pay problems, dealing with urgent Red Cross messages, arranging emergency leave, coordinating casualty evacuations, or providing legal assistance, Misty was informed on what they were dealing with. "The dedication of Marines, who willingly put their lives on the line for others, whether they served four years or forty, inspired me every single day. Being able to make a real difference in their lives, that's where I knew I belonged—and as an Adjutant, I knew I could do just that."

As time passed, Misty felt a strong pull back to Marine Corps Recruit Depot Parris Island. "I had once walked through those gates as an enlisted Marine, a recruit, and now I yearned to return as a Series Commander. As a Mustang—having transitioned from enlisted to officer—I brought a unique perspective to the role of Series Commander. I knew firsthand what it meant to stand in the shoes of a recruit, staring at my footlocker. I wanted to stand beside those extraordinary 18-year-old women, knowing that they could have chosen any path, yet they bravely chose to be there."

"Marine Corps Recruit Depot isn't for the faint-hearted. These young women were asked to do what many only dream of having the courage to attempt. Walking through the squad bay, I felt the weight of responsibility knowing that I was the embodiment of what an Officer represents in the Marine Corps. Facing 120 eager women, all aspiring to be part of an organization, is a humbling experience. It's a reminder that once you're a part of the Marine Corps, you're a part of it for life. Standing among these remarkable young Americans, who embody the essence of what it means to be American, is an incredibly powerful position to be in."

# THE TRANSITION

"I can vividly recall the moment when I made the decision about my post-uniform career path. It was at the 15-year mark of my service, during my tenure at the Special Projects Directorate office, where we organized events for the Senior Leadership of the Marine Corp such as Executive Off-Sites. Our responsibilities also extended to coordinating Marine Week, Fleet Week, and Foreign Counterpart Visits."

Misty found herself at the Navy Yard in Washington DC, overseeing a Retired Executive Off-Site (REOS) event attended by a recently retired General whom she had seen transition out of service a few months prior. "Engaging in conversation, I inquired about his post-military transition and the hurdles he faced. As he shared his challenges, I realized that many mirrored the administrative tasks I had performed for our Generals while in uniform. In that moment, clarity struck. I knew what I was meant to do next."

Inspired by the realization, Misty envisioned creating a support system akin to the General Staff offices but tailored for retired Generals. "My goal was to provide them with the necessary support to leverage their expertise and continue contributing to the national security sector. Despite leaving active service, these men and women still have a desire to serve and make an impact, yet they require assistance with certain business aspects. I recognized that I could offer this support."

"I understood my purpose and the community I aimed to serve." She launched her company and dedicated it to assisting retiring general and flag officers in establishing their consultancy businesses and furnishing them with executive support to optimize their operations. "They still require support, and if I continue to do what I am good at and they do the same, our nation benefits from it. With 35 to 40 years of invaluable experience, these remarkable individuals remain committed to giving back to private industry, offering unique perspectives, strategic planning abilities, and distinctive leadership styles."

Says Misty, "With me, they find a sanctuary where unspoken understanding prevails. As fellow veterans who have served together, we share a deep bond—I know their capabilities, and they understand my role implicitly. There's no need for elaborate explanations; we simply understand. This mutual familiarity allows me to articulate their value clearly to other organizations and negotiate fees on their behalf. I recognize the extraordinary leadership, expertise, and invaluable lessons they bring, qualities that cannot be bought or taught in any degree program. Their unique experiences and the lessons learned during a 35+ year career shape them into exceptional assets for our private industry partners."

## LESSONS LEARNED

Make decisions that will stand the test of time. "Many times, I faced circumstances that weren't handled as I believed they should have been. Despite the difficulties, I remained steadfast in my actions, knowing that I did everything I could do. Looking back, I take pride in how I handled that trying period, recognizing that integrity and treating others with respect are enduring principles. Avoid the temptation of comfort-driven choices and strive to be the kind of person you'd admire ten years down the road."

## WHAT'S NEXT

Misty continues to expand her clientele base. "I'm privileged to support remarkable leaders as they embark on the next phase of their lives. This is their time to strike a balance between work and family, often relishing moments with their grandchildren. My aim is to alleviate the challenges of entrepreneurship and accelerate their progress."

To achieve this, Misty has devised a comprehensive 16-week roadmap, guiding them through the establishment of essential business components, development strategies, and sustainable growth frameworks. "Throughout this journey, I provide coaching on self-valuation and personal branding as expert consultants." Additionally, during this program and even after its conclusion, she remains dedicated to providing ongoing executive support to these individuals. "I take charge of all administrative processes, freeing them from these burdens and allowing them to focus on optimizing their business endeavors."

# THE MILITARY EFFECT

"One of the most important things I have been a part of following retirement is serving as the Military Protocol Consultant for The Marine Corps Memorial Foundation in Denver, CO. Spearheaded by our fearless President, Ms. Paula Sarls—a dedicated Marine Corps Veteran and Gold Star Spouse—the Foundation has been relentless in its fundraising endeavors. My utmost desire is to rally support and encourage others to join us in our mission to complete the remodel project. Together, we aim to restore the Marine Corps Memorial to its rightful place of dignity and honor, paying tribute to the noble service of the Marine Corps and its members."

# 35

## MOLLY JENKS, ARMY

linkedin.com/in/molly-j-2202347
**Hometown:** *Tuscon, Arizona*
**Currently Resides:** *Washington, D.C.*

## WHY I SERVED

An Army Brat growing up, it never occurred to Molly not to join the military. "I loved the aspect of moving all the time, living in other countries, and the teamwork aspect of the military. Some people run to it and some run from it. I was definitely one of those 'run to it' kind of people. When my dad moved, we moved. His main priority was the family first and keeping us all together as a single unit."

"A big trigger for me was my brother going to West Point. It really opened my eyes." Molly visited while he was there, unsure yet if she wanted to serve. She applied to all the academies and was accepted into the Prep Schools for both the Naval Academy and West Point. "Both services bring so much to the table in such vastly different ways. Honestly, I sat on it for a week or so before accepting the offer for Army. It was the best choice I ever made." She soon blew out her knee, no longer physically qualified. The next stop was Xavier where Molly joined ROTC and swam competitively and studied Biochemistry. Molly was commissioned as a Signal lieutenant and halfway through her career was selected to Advanced Civil Schooling and earned her mMaster's Degree in Nuclear Physics. "I didn't think I would be in the military for long and planned to get a job in the medical field after. As soon as I got in, I loved it and told myself I would stop when it wasn't fun anymore." Her Army career lasted 20 years.

Preparing for Officer Basic Course (OBC), Molly's dad would wake her up every morning at 4:30am with reveille and to go running. "I would tell him to leave me alone, but he persisted. I hated running." It was years before she learned her father felt the same way about running, but believed in quality time and instilling a hard work ethic of pushing out of your comfort zone was critical for both personal and professional success.

Faced with multiple challenges throughout her career, two of the most difficult times arose while Molly was a Commander. She was based in Sadr City, Baghdad from April 03-August 04. "The military had a strict 365-day deployment rule. Since WW II, no troops were to be deployed longer than 365 days continuously. On 4 April 2004 everything changed. We were set to redeploy, and I found out on Yahoo News my entire unit was extended indefinitely.

Soon after returning from Iraq, one of Molly's Soldiers tragically drowned while off duty with his friends. With proper notifications made, Molly took leave and flew back to the United States pay her respects to the family in person. "My soldier was the son of an Army Senior Non-Commissioned Officer, and I was the Commander. I was responsible for keeping people under my Command safe, and I had failed with his son." Showing up to the house, Molly was fully prepared to feel the brunt of the family's anger over losing their son. "Instead, the first thing his father told me was that they believed it was incredible that their son's mother was also named Mollie. He came into this world with a Mollie who loved and cared for him, and he left this world with a Molly who loved and cared for him." The family and Molly are in touch to this day many times a year. They have celebrated many milestones together, including Molly's retirement and the family opening a new ministry.

## THE TRANSITION

Molly's retirement was emotional and rewarding. Someone in her family had served on active duty from WWII, until her retirement. At the ceremony, generations of her family and soldiers from every position during her career flew in to celebrate. Soon after retiring, Molly was home one night relaxing. "I was literally sitting at dinner with, at that time, the current Chief of Staff of the Army, General George Casey and his wife Sheila. He said, 'So, what are you going to do now, Molly?'. Nothing, I'm tired and need a break." That lasted about 30 days. His wife Sheila joked that he also needed a break and should heed one of his troops' advice."

A posting on social media ended her 'vacation'. "I had a picture on there of our brigade combat team. A colleague who served with me saw it needed a liaison officer for his company. He was like, 'Hey Molly, I noticed you are retiring. Come work for me'." She continues, "I said sure. The thing about being a nuclear officer is trying to explain complex situations down to a less complex level, and it was perfect for this role as a liaison."

Molly soon set her sights on the prestigious firm Booz Allen. "I thought it would be a good fit for my Communications Officer and Nuclear Advisor. Some of my military skills transferred over seamlessly. I had served as LTG Honore's Communications advisor during Hurricane Katrina, so I was used to briefing Senior level leaders in tense, lifesaving situations." As a Nuclear Disablement Team Chief and also advising foreign governments on UN Security Resolution's, Molly had tremendous experience working with several different Governmental and civilian organizations. "With Booz Allen, I have been fortunate to serve the Chief of Naval Operations (CNO), The Department of Defense Senior Communications Officer, and advising on Nuclear Command, Control and Communications (NC3) with the Joint Staff."

Taking this leap of faith from the strict regimen of the military to a more fluid environment like Booz Allen had its challenges. "I was used to being told every aspect of my life, from doctors I was allowed to see, to the exact diameter of earring I was authorized to wear (7mm for those curious). Booz Allen was 180 degrees from that lifestyle, down to their recommendation of "Dress for the Day. Many veterans have a difficult time transitioning, and I was no different. The best advice I received was to be patient, be kind to yourself, and find a job that is the right fit for you."

## LESSONS LEARNED

You are never too good. You are never above anything. Always be of service to others. Even when you are having a rough time, appreciate what you DO have, and strive to help others.

## WHAT'S NEXT

On March 31st, 2020, Molly was diagnosed with MEITL (Non-Hodgkin Lymphoma). It was aggressive, and no previous survivors were known to even have been treated. After consulting with both Sloane Kettering and Walter Reed, the decision was made to treat her with a stem cell transplant. "I'm much better now, and even got to meet my donor. I have taken on properties from her that are fascinating. My blood type changed from B to A, I don't get bitten by mosquitos, and I now have two distinctly different DNAs in my body."

Molly is back at work full time working on NATO exercises and sensors for better detection of WMD events. She is also passionate about animals and is now fostering rottweiler dogs. "I want to give back, and dogs are so great. Recently, I got to meet President Bush's service dog, Sully." She also volunteers at NIH Children's Hospital. "They were so good to me. My sickness was rough, but it's toughest with kids."

She also is a vocal advocate for stem cell treatment. Says Molly, "There is a huge lack of minority representation in the "library" for donors, with little being stored. I want to increase awareness to be a stem cell donor to save someone's life, helping to bridge the gap between minority groups and government efforts."

So thankful for her recovery, Molly brings together friends each anniversary. This year she has invited fifteen of her closest friends to celebrate her 50th birthday in the Turks and Cacaos. "This disease is a chapter of my life, but not the whole book."

## THE MILITARY EFFECT

"I just had a really great time being in different countries, different cities, different states, every year to four years. And meeting new people while learning about their customs and cultures was absolutely fascinating. We live and work in a global community, learning about our differences and similarities only makes us more respectful and understanding of everyone."

# 36

## NEAL CONLON, MARINES

linkedin.com/in/nealconlon
**Hometown:** *Queens, New York*
**Currently Resides:** *Fishkill, New York*

## WHY I SERVED

Neil grew up in Queens, raised by his mom. With very little direction from parental figures he says, "I had really, really great grandfathers. They were just these men of high value and high integrity. And my grandmothers shared their immigrant values that hard work pays off. When I got into my teenage years, I was really attracted to that concept." Getting his first job at 13, Neal has been working ever since.

After being an unruly young man and being kicked out of several schools and not wanting to go to college, Neal was hanging out at school one day and noticed a couple of Marine Corps recruiters. "I was like, look at these guys. I watched a couple of videos on my own about it and was drawn to patriotism and how they had such purpose" He continues, "I really wanted to get out of New York and see the world. I wanted to jump out of helicopters and blow things up." Neal signed up on his 18th birthday. That night he went home and told mom over dinner, "I joined the Marine Corps, and I will leave in three months."

## THE TRANSITION

His plan was to do a full 20 years in Marine Corps. "When I went in, I wanted to go to the warrant officer program and had my package submitted to headquarters Marine Corps." Married at a young age, and living in a topsy-turvy relationship with multiple deployments, he was getting burnt out. "As I picked up rank, I kept meeting senior enlisted who were kind of institutionalized. It was so life changing to experience leaders being afraid to move forward. knew it was time to leave."

For about 10 years, Neal didn't want to talk about service or wear the shirt or even a sticker. "I actually wrote a blog about 12 years ago called, 'The Day I Didn't Have to Be a Marine'. After that first 10 years, even though I wasn't drawn to that veteran story or narrative, every single job interview I ever went to they asked about my background, and I started with 'I'm a Marine Corps veteran'."

Neil's first job was as a security guard. "The building that I was in was 135 East 57th Street and the reason why it's important is because that is the building where they put all of the post 9/11 World Trade Center financial services offices, so its security was extremely high." In about six months he realized that there had to be more for him and wrote his first resume, taking it floor to floor in the building and handing the resume to every HR person. "I didn't know what a hedge fund was or what assets under management were or anything like that." One of the people Neil handed the resume to was Brian Sir, the global Chief Operating Officer of Guggenheim Partners. He said, "I don't know what we're going to do with you, but we're going to hire you."

Starting in the mail room, he was soon given more duties, learning fast. "I had to be taught about efficiency and how to both manage and respond to email." One day Neil found out that the interns were making twice his pay. He quit and was immediately recruited to Cushman, Wakefield working for the CEO who had a soft spot in his heart for veterans. "I got pulled into the inner circles, meeting with some of the richest and most powerful decision makers in the country. I started to really just take all these leadership principles and the leadership doctrine of the Marine Corps and wondered how to apply it to what I do, so it's not this hyper-aggressive masculine thing."

His entry point into networking started with MeetUp. "In 2009, I made a commitment to meet three new people a day and did it for a year. I didn't care who it was as long as I felt like they had something that I could learn or contribute to me. It was a huge foundational piece in my career, from interns to investors to entrepreneurs. and I still speak to many of these peers and have often been referred to as a master connector because of the depth and width of my network."

## LESSONS LEARNED

Authenticity only comes with trust and community.

## WHAT'S NEXT

Neil is now a business and mindset coach that guides Fortune 500 executives and veterans to change their frame of mind. 'The transition for many is like going from being the apex predator in the organization to just being an average everyday guy in the street." He pulls lots of his content from his military background. "A lot of my framework and structure methodology stuff is really coming out of the organizational structures in the military." One of his clients is a Fortune 500 company, retraining them in accountability.

"When I coach there are two phases. The first one is the transition phase, where I help executives and veterans unlearn some of their prior experience. The second phase of it is when they have a business idea, and they want to set the business up so they can actually seek some form of real investment." Neil adds, "I have very strong feelings that while I probably don't have an alternative solution at the moment, I think a lot of those programs really limit military veterans' thought processes for how you're going to go from zero to a million dollars."

A strong proponent of networking, Neil utilizes LinkedIn. "I use it every day." He believes in being very authentic, very clear, very intentional, very helpful, and very to the point. "I've integrated that into my life in a way that for a lot of people. It's a hard thing for them to take the wrapping paper off of a military veteran. There is a congruence in the military that seems to fade into civilian life, and I love coaching people to their new congruence."

Neil recently started competing in endurance and Ironman events. To expand his training schedule, he pivoted his coaching business into the Fortune 500 space for greater revenue. "I didn't think it would elevate so fast." He's coached executives and has done keynote speeches for companies like Bausch and Lomb, Bristol Myers Squib and Cintas. "In 2024, we launched a full-scale program called OMNIS, which is Latin for all. The DNA of it is relational networking, radical accountability and enhanced support and services all in one platform." In addition, he offers a group coaching program for supporting people to step into their greatness.

## THE MILITARY EFFECT

Neal realizes how hard it is for veterans when they go back home into the workplace. "There is a limiting belief that if you don't talk to someone with a military background, they won't see what you are capable of." He adds, "There are a lot of cool veteran organizations like Vets in Tech, based in Silicon Valley that combines veterans and technology.'" He also has connections with American Dream U and Bunker Labs. "I even found a Facebook group specifically for veteran entrepreneurs called Vetpreneur Tribe and Warrior Rising. All of these programs create scaffolding. But I'm convinced that there needs to be better vehicles for integration back into civilian life."

# 37

## PATRICK GEORGE, MARINES

linkedin.com/in/patrickgeorge
**Hometown:** *Dallas, Texas*
**Currently Resides:** *Puerto Rico*

### WHY I SERVED

Studying at the University of Texas at Austin, Patrick's original plan was to serve his country working with Teach for America. "I come from a family with a military and political history. We were raised that you serve your country in some form or fashion." But after 9/11 and the ramp-up in '03, he decided to wear the uniform instead. "I thought, what better way to develop my leadership skills straight out of undergrad than to be on the front lines?"

Patrick's father served with the 82nd Airborne during Vietnam. "He always told me, 'If you don't want to be on a boat, don't join the Navy. If you don't want to fly, don't join the Air Force. And whatever you do, don't join the Army.'" This process of elimination led Patrick to the Marine Corps recruiting office. "I told them I don't need the pitch, just give me the paperwork."

The Marine Corps had recently developed a program called Platoon Leaders Course (PLC), which allowed you to attend bootcamp during the summer while finishing your undergraduate degree. "I'll never forget writing letters home to mom saying, 'This is like summer camp with guns. I love it. And so, I finished my two degrees and signed on the dotted line. I knew I was going to war, so all I was focused on was becoming the best infantry officer I could be."

Patrick completed two combat tours to Iraq, "I had gone through my first combat tour. as a platoon commander, which was an incredible experience. After screening for MARSOC at A&S, I finished my second tour as the Operations Officer managing the western border of Iraq." Patrick turned down the opportunity to return to MARSOC and moved into the Inactive Ready Reserve. "Honestly, I thought I was done." As fate would have it, and weeks away from resigning his commission, Patrick was randomly introduced to the Inspector Instructor for 4th Recon Battalion. After one conversation, Patrick submitted his paperwork just days before the cutoff and rejoined the Marine Corps Reserve.

## THE TRANSITION

In 2010, the war in Iraq looked like it was ending, and Patrick wasn't getting excited about a new five-year commitment. "I was single, no kids, and would be sent to the East Coast. I felt like it was time to transition into a civilian career, get a graduate degree in finance, and enter the business world." He transitioned into the Inactive Ready Reserve and headed to Cornell for an MBA.

Patrick was raised in Dallas, but his family is from the heart of oil and gas country, the Permian. After finishing his graduate degree, he jumped into the industry immediately. "It is a global commodity, and I love how energy involves geopolitics, national security, entrepreneurship, and where your reputation and handshake matter."

After a few years in investment banking, Patrick decided to build his own company, focusing on what he knew best: west Texas oil and gas. His entrepreneurial journey had started with a bit of fear and uncertainty. "I met some great people who gave me the confidence to get started, assuring me I could absolutely do it. It had a huge impact." In less than three years, his company was making millions in revenue and seeing great success.

For Patrick, one of the tools that helped him immensely was social media. "I didn't appreciate it until I was at The Basic School in the Marine Corps. Don't forget, back in the early 2000s, there was only Facebook and MySpace." He found LinkedIn to be incredibly powerful in building a network. "It's allowed me to get my message out when I'm trying to push content and support causes, I'm passionate about."

## LESSONS LEARNED

A smart man learns from his mistakes, but a wise man learns from the mistakes of others.

## WHAT'S NEXT

"I've always wanted to live in a Latin culture and learn other languages." In '21, Patrick moved to Puerto Rico with a duffel bag, briefcase, and his two dogs. "I initially wanted to try it out for a year and have loved it. Last year, I bought a house."

Patrick is still in the reserves and part of a disaggregated unit. "We are stationed everywhere, even though our base is in New York." All of the same requirements as a reservist apply, so he maintains the annual requirements while working remotely. "I hope to get promoted and either command a ground unit or serve internationally."

On the business front, things remain positive. "I love the venture capital space and have transitioned more into green energy." Patrick's company, Hover Energy, is now on three continents with plans to move further into Europe. One of his investments, UpSmith, is helping to attract veterans and put them through a trade program.

## THE MILITARY EFFECT

"Help me understand as a civilian how your military background transcribes to the job that you're interviewing for. We don't teach service members how to do that. What do you wear to an interview? I mean, I've had guys show up to interviews wearing sweatpants and I'm like, 'Guys, you're not going to get the job.' Frankly, when we leave the military, we don't have a lot of money to buy a professional wardrobe that you now have to purchase for yourself."

## 38

## ROBERT HAMILTON OWENS, AIR FORCE

linkedin.com/in/robert-hamilton-owens-6a6a9493
**Hometown:** *Anaheim, California*
**Currently Resides:** *Newport Beach, California*

## WHY I SERVED

The product of war-time Marine Pilot and Navy wife affair, Robert was placed in a baby orphanage in Orange, California far away from San Diego where they both lived. "I was there for three months. I was a special-needs baby and had a number of physical challenges with my feet and ankles. For six years I wore Forrest Gump type braces and shoes on my legs. I didn't learn to run unaided until I was in sixth grade."

Robert grew up near water boogie boarding, skim boarding, and surfing. He was always being encouraged by his mother, who was a graduate of UCLA in physical education. In High School, he played water polo under John Urbanchek, a legendary ex-Hungarian Olympian. "When you are a swimmer in Southern California, often you become ocean beach lifeguards." It was his love for the water that landed Robert a position as one before his 16th birthday. He had to get a waiver from the city to work that summer.

"At 20 years old, I listened to two Pararescue Reservists from the 303rd Reserve Unit at March Air Force Base in Riverside California. They were San Clemente Lifeguards on weekends when they were home. They told me that I was smart and had a ton of talent but that I was undisciplined and too lazy to accomplish anything in life. They told me I ought to come in and become a USAF Pararescueman like them. I said OK. I'll join the Air Force." That was 1972.

Robert went in the Active Duty Military in March 1973. "We had over 150 kids tryout. After thirteen weeks of what we called 'InDoc', which is short for Indoctrination, ten of us graduated along with six rollbacks. They made me Team Leader for our 13-month 'Pipeline Training'." He served for four years until the Air Force told each of the nine Pararescue units in the world that there was going to be budget cuts after the Vietnam war. Each Unit had to downsize by 20% in four months. "I was low man with 'in-service time' in my Unit in 1978 and was asked to leave the Air Force. I wished many times that I've been allowed to stay longer."

## THE TRANSITION

"When I knew I was going to have to get out, I began to look for Post Service plans." Four months after getting out of service, Robert began to smuggle Christian literature into the Soviet Union and smuggled political NATO documents out. "This was during the Carter administration when the Russians were violating a number of NATO agreements concerning the SS 22 nuclear missiles." It was also a reflection time for Robert to figure out what he really wanted to do with his life.

Robert entered Theology school when he wasn't smuggling. "After graduation, I went to the University of Nevada-Reno where I became Chaplain for football, baseball, and basketball for the next 25 years working with students and athletes." Being a little bit bored with church work, he soon started a Leadership Training Consulting Business. "I begin to do staff management and leadership training for a number of businesses and companies."

That consulting work opened the door for Robert to work in over thirty nations around the world, teaching, coaching, and consulting. "I made sixteen trips to Africa and South Africa, ten trips to Moscow, and twelve trips to Beijing doing underground pro-democracy work."

## LESSONS LEARNED

I wouldn't be where I am today in my life if it wasn't for the coaches who pushed me.

## WHAT'S NEXT

"After I got out, I found that I enjoyed staying in shape. That led to being one of the original Ironman Triathletes before it was called Ironman. Over the years that led to 12 Ironman Triathlons, 20 Marathons, 6 Half Ironman's, running the World Marathon Challenge or 777: 7 Marathons in 7 Days on 7 Continents and other endurance events." Robert was most recently on a European Rowing team that rowed across the Atlantic Ocean. The trip took 43 days to row 3200 miles.

Today, Robert occasionally trains Air Force Special Warfare Active-Duty personnel at Lackland Air Force Base in San Antonio, Texas. He is also a paid coach for SEALFIT.com. This organization trains Navy SEAL, Army Ranger, MARSOC as well as Air Force Special Ops trainees. " I've been doing that now for six years."

The program is legendary. Says Robert, "We have a 6-hour, 12-hour, 24-hour and 50-hour nonstop basic intro training crucible." Each is with Navy SEAL coaches, except for Robert. "It is designed to replicate the first 50 hours of Hell Week in BUDS." Robert is the oldest to have ever finished the 50-hour nonstop Crucible Event. "I did it at 66 years old. I wanted to see if I could get in the same shape in my 60's as I had been in my 20's." After completing it, he was asked to be the only non-Navy SEAL coach.

"I really enjoy working with young men and women who have big dreams and who want to do huge things. We try to instill in them confidence and skills to accomplish the goals that they've set for themselves." Three years ago, they had a young man from Ohio come to the 50-hour nonstop experience at 16 years old for his Senior High School Graduation Project. Says Robert, "He did really well. Three weeks ago, I went to his Navy SEAL graduation where he graduated at nineteen as the youngest in his class."

Robert is also a recruited member of the Adventure Club of Los Angeles, which Teddy Roosevelt started in 1912 for adventurers. "I get invited all the time to go spend time with these adventure types all over the world. I now have a fifty-year endurance career. I get paid to talk about my adventures as well as my mistakes."

## THE MILITARY EFFECT

In one of Robert's many athletic achievements, rowing the Atlantic took on a special meaning. "We lost one of our instructors at SEALFIT to suicide. So, I decided to do this competition and raise awareness and funds to stop this horrific trend." It became a documentary called 'One is Too Many', 43 Days, 3000 miles. Rowing for the Lives of our Veterans (www.oneistoomanyfilm.com).

# 39

## SAL FILARDI, ARMY

linkedin.com/in/sal-filardi
**Hometown:** *New Haven, Connecticut*
**Currently Resides:** *West Chester, Pennsylvania*

### WHY I SERVED

Sal attended an all-boy's private high school, Marmion Academy. Formerly a military school, he and nearly 90% of students participated in Army JROTC. Later, at the University of Illinois, Sal struggled with the lack of structure and felt lost. Sal heard about the university's ROTC program, which offered a tuition waiver. "It sounded like a chance to do something I was already good at and pay for school while doing it". Ironically, on his first day, he got in trouble after correcting an upperclassman's form on a technique he'd done innumerable times on his high school Drill Team. The structure was back, for better or worse.

"My senior year, I was ranked dead last in my ROTC class." A coveted active-duty assignment wasn't even on his radar. But a new senior instructor had just arrived. He decided to form his own opinion of Sal and was impressed by his accomplishments outside of ROTC. "In hindsight, I learned by his example to focus on the team you have and help them become their best." Near graduation, an unexpected opening came down from headquarters. "He pulled me into his office and explained the incredible opportunity, a chance to join his former branch. I moved to Oklahoma and began training 5 days after earning a diploma."

Sal was energized. "It was the first time I concentrated all my efforts into one thing, and I started crushing it." His unit was sent to Korea; his first time leaving the country. "As a sheltered midwestern kid, it was easy to assume the American way is the best and only way. To see Korean artillerymen whose everyday lives depend on their ability to defend their northern border changed my perspective and made me want to work with foreign militaries in the future."

While there, many of Sal's close friends tried to become Green Berets. He started to learn about the Special Forces and entered the selection process as soon as he got back stateside. "I knew the odds were extremely slim and that I didn't have several of the traditional attributes of successful candidates. It was effectively a hail-Mary. I worked my butt off in order to be average. It was the most impressive group of people I've ever met." At the end of the month-long ordeal, Sal made the cut.

"I think the military is 50% luck and 50% timing. I tried it out in 2017, showed an aptitude for foreign language, and served in the Pacific - a hot spot at the time". After the two-year Special Forces Qualification Course, Sal arrived at 3rd Special Forces Group when the wars in the Middle East came to an abrupt halt. "I ended up serving in Africa, not Afghanistan like I had imagined. My team focused on training and advisory missions in West Africa. It was an incredible experience and I hope I get to go back to those countries in the future."

## THE TRANSITION

"The Honor Foundation was the launchpad for my transition. One of the many things they helped with was telling my story without relying on military jargon." Creating a resume was a challenge. He contemplated the question of how you take the theme of service and continue it in the private sector. "You chuckle when you see some of the requirements on job postings because you are simultaneously over and under qualified."

Sal started by choosing the path of the solo entrepreneur and became a certified Pinnacle Business Guide, helping businesses create alignment and best practices for leadership teams. To get more involved in the local community, he started teaching golf with First Tee. "I love teaching kids. It's one of the hardest challenges for communication, clarity, and empathy."

"I was focused on finding new opportunities and building my network". He took advantage of several groups for veterans (Med Tech Vets & Vets in Tech), along with tons of outreach on LinkedIn. "It was the bridge between my connections that led to me creating the opportunities that I was most excited about."

## LESSONS LEARNED

Leaders are Learners first - traveling the world professionally forced me to constantly view my team, my processes, and my idea of success from new angles. We were constantly adapting and improving because of it.

## WHAT'S NEXT

Less than a year out of the military, at the time of publishing, Sal is shifting from a wide search to a narrow focus. "After a few hundred reps of introducing myself, I started to realize that the closest comparison to the Green Berets in the private sector is strategy and management consulting. Coincidentally, that industry is perfect for swapping proficiency in military tactics for financial acumen and business analytics."

Sal is an associate at GreenCastle Consulting where he combines his past experience with new certifications in Lean 6 Sigma, Scrum, Agile, Project Management, and Change Management to help businesses execute their most ambitious initiatives.

In the near future, he plans to continue his education by pursuing an MBA. Ultimately, he would like to influence at the intersection of healthcare and technology at a Venture Capital or Private Equity firm, returning to an industry whose ripples can make positive impacts globally.

## THE MILITARY EFFECT

"One thing you might not consider if the only Green Beret you know is Rambo, hides in our creed: 'Teach & Fight'. That order is purposeful and powerful. We exist to teach, influence, and understand how complex and foreign problems change the game. When your team only has 12 people, you have to figure out what's at the center of the multi-circle Venn diagram and put pressure right there."

## 40

## SHANNON POTTS, MARINES

linkedin.com/in/shannon-potts-496a8544
**Hometown:** *Algonquin, Illinois*
**Currently Resides:** *Tampa, Florida*

## WHY I SERVED

In eighth grade, Shannon vividly remembers seeing the dress blue uniform on Marines in posters and commercials. "My stepdad was a former Marine and he shared information about his time in the Marines. When we went to fairs, I would see the recruiters in their uniforms, and it caught my eye right away. I knew I wanted to be a part of that."

Shannon got in touch with a recruiter at her high school. "It was the spring of 2001, and I didn't have a way to pay for college, nor did I feel ready for college. I knew the Marine Corps was an avenue and was ready to join." She continues, "The values of honor, courage and commitment resonated with me. I asked my recruiter if I could sign for twenty years right then. He told me that's not how it works. Four years at a time. I wanted to be a career Marine."

She enlisted, entered boot camp in January 2002 and a few years in, submitted her officer package. "Aside from the travel and education benefits, this was a way to contribute to something bigger than myself." Once commissioned, Shannon became an Adjutant, stepping away from the aviation community into administration. "I really learned what it means to serve; my position as an officer meant I was there to take care of these Marines."

## THE TRANSITION

"I was on my first contract as an officer, having commissioned in October of 2009. I was at the juncture in 2013 where I decided that it was time to exit the Marine Corps, and I declined career designation." Shannon was expecting her fourth child, and her husband was working out of state. "It became quite challenging to find that work/life balance, and I wanted to support my husband's job. I left the Marine Corps to be a stay-at-home mom."

Being a stay-at-home mom felt harder than being a Marine some days. "The Marine Corps was all I knew in my adult life to that point. That was where my identity came from." Shannon tried the Reserves for six months, and it was still a balance and a juggle. "My husband would fly home, watch the kids while I flew to Minnesota to go to drill, and then we were high fiving on the way back. It was not what I wanted for our family, so I dropped to the Individual Ready Reserve and was a civilian for three years. In that time, we had our fifth child, and he was born requiring lots of medical attention bringing us on quite the medical journey."

Shannon was contacted by a prior service recruiter in late 2016. "While initially expressing no interest in returning to the Marine Corps, with the support of my husband and children, I joined 1st Battalion, 23d Marine Regiment out of Houston, Texas for three and a half years. It was very rewarding." She relished the challenge of going back. "I still had that desire to serve, and I love being around Marines."

In 2020, she was selected to attend professional military education at Army Command and General Staff College in Fort Leavenworth, Kansas, having her 6th child while in school. Shannon's journey has been anything but typical, as she has been active and Reserve multiple times. "During the transition from active duty to civilian life, I got involved in groups at a church in Texas and still participate in Bible study online. It's been an important part of my life." She continues, "I also found community through joining CrossFit. I have learned over time that finding those communities and those networks is so important. And that is exactly what I try to share with my Marines too."

## LESSONS LEARNED

Get everybody's collective feedback so that they feel like they have that buy in. It makes the team stronger.

## WHAT'S NEXT

Currently stationed in San Bruno, California with 23d Marine Regiment, 4th Marine Division, Shannon was offered career designation in the Active Reserve program; she accepted this time. Shannon says, "Right now, life is really jam-packed, and we are awaiting orders for our next duty station. There's a lot to think about as we plan for the future. After this summer, I'll have four years left to be eligible for retirement. With six kids, I want to be present in their lives."

As Shannon considers all options, she shares, "One day, I absolutely want to be more involved in the CrossFit community; maybe own an affiliate gym. The CrossFit CEO, Don Faul, is a former Marine. Hopefully I can meet him, network and talk about his journey into CrossFit." Shannon and her brother, also a Marine, have big dreams of buying a ranch with a ton of land. "He can have a smoothie shop or a restaurant, and I'll run camps for kids, or veterans transitioning or military spouses; lots to think about."

# THE MILITARY EFFECT

"While still immersed in military life but working at an independent duty station rather than near a large military installation, I get to interact with the community in ways I had not while on active duty. It's exciting and rewarding. It feels like it has come full circle; I saw Marines at fairs or during the holiday season for Toys for Tots growing up, and now I get to participate in many community relation events. I get to represent the Marine Corps and its values now in the Bay Area. It's important to see the faces and know what we look like and the communities that we live in."

## 41

## STACY RASKE, ARMY

linkedin.com/in/stacyraske
**Hometown:** *Chicago, Illinois*
**Currently Resides:** *Tampa, Florida*

## WHY I SERVED

Growing up, Stacy was accustomed to moving around a lot. But at age 16 she had had enough. "My mom said we were moving again. I was done with that. Being homeless, I ended up couch surfing with friends to finish high school. She followed the traditional path into college, but then decided to take a break and move to Utah.

"I always knew the military would be part of my life. In February of 2021 I walked into the Army recruiter's office. I was 22 and ready for a change in my life". Says Stacy, "Being a science nerd, I wanted to do something in that field, so I chose Chemical Operations. Once in, I was selected for Biowarfare Detection School." Waiting for her assignment in Salt Lake City, she watched the events unfold on 9/11. A few days later her unit was deployed to the Pentagon to clean up anthrax. "We were the first unit since the Civil War to have an official stateside, war-time deployment."

## THE TRANSITION

Stationed in Iraq, Stacy worked closely with the Marines, convoying all over the country. "I got hurt on one of my missions and didn't know how bad it was till the PT test after returning home." After being medically discharged, she moved to Pennsylvania with her husband, recently celebrating their 20th wedding anniversary. "We met at Biowarfare Detection School and served together at the Pentagon."

Relocating was not easy. She didn't know anyone. "Being a disabled veteran, I decided to go back to college." This was the start of a new journey, and one that has taken almost 10 years.

"Why is it so hard to transition out? Because you lose the community you built and have to start all over again. It sometimes felt like a trauma recovery journey with a stream of triggers setting things off." Says Stacy, "I had to learn boundaries, which is a skill set I never learned and why I was getting burned out." She found coaches, mentors and teachers to learn what she needed.

Says Stacy, "I'm happy to now be with my tribe. It took a while to get here but I now know who I am."

## LESSONS LEARNED

Your community helps you thrive after service.

## WHAT'S NEXT?

"I'm very thoughtful about who I have in my network and the different layers of my bubble. This helps me attract a whole new wave of high-level, empowered entrepreneurial veterans to do business with."

Stacy has connected with amazing entrepreneurs through various groups, mastermind communities and events she's attended. "It's curating the people who I connect with on a multi-layered dynamic. Building a lifestyle that integrates and harmonizes all of it." She goes on to say, "If we can do life and business and impact and leadership and all the things together, that for me is a fulfilling relationship because it checks so many aspects of what's important."

This year she's focused on creating space. "I've been casual in my online presence. I'm still networking organically, but it's not my primary strategy for growth. Connecting with people directly is so much faster and provides greater ROI." Stacy prefers this over the "spray and pray method'" of traditional networking that often ends up purely transactional.

"I'm open to the spontaneity of new opportunities coming in." Her next phase of business will include another book, a television project and strategic network growth. Says Stacy, "I have big vision and big goals. WHO I engage with is so important to achieve them."

## THE MILITARY EFFECT

She is happy to be part of Business Beyond the Battlefield(https://bbbc. uta.edu/). It's a conference designed to help veterans, and those interested in the community. "I have been many times. The networking is amazing, and connecting with both veterans and business leaders is so rewarding." Stacy hopes to go next year and continues to share with other veterans.

# 42

## SUZANNE LESKO, NAVY

linkedin.com/in/suzannelesko
**Hometown:** *Pittsburgh, Pennsylvania*
**Currently Resides:** *Naples, Florida*

## WHY I SERVED

First, because it was in her blood. Her father served in the U.S. Air Force, and her grandparents also served, and the expectation was that Suzanne, and her sister would explore this opportunity as well. Second, being a small-town girl from the steel city of Pittsburgh, PA (Go Steelers and Penguins!), she had a strong desire to see the world and what it had to offer.

Suzanne remembers in 1991 as a high school athlete (she loved swimming, track, and golf) being approached by a Blue & Gold Officer (B&GO). He told her that he was scouting candidates for the U.S. Naval Academy (USNA). Unfortunately, he did it while she was taking a swing on the golf course and her response was, "FORE!!!!"

Suzanne and her older sister looked at and visited other academies. This presented a quandary for her. She the opportunity to go to TWO very prestigious academies – the U.S. Naval Academy in Annapolis, or the U.S. Military Academy at West Point – along with other Ivy League colleges. She'd like to say that she did a lot of in-depth research, but remember, this was 1991 and internet searches were not a thing; there was no Google or even Ask Jeeves. In the end, the B&GO was a major influence in Suzanne's decision to apply to the U.S. Naval Academy, as he addressed a lot of her questions and concerns.

Upon entering the Navy, at the tender age of eighteen, Suzanne was thrown in at the deep end. She describes it this way, "I underwent INTENSE training, firstly at the Quigley, as a midshipman in Quantico, Virginia and then as part of level-C of the Survival, Evasion, Resistance, and Escape (SERE) program for high-risk-of-capture military personnel." During active service, she flew counter-drug missions in Central and South America and overland missions in other parts of the world, as well as experiencing combat in Iraq from 2007 to 2009. She led and directed large-scale campaigns, missions, operations, and teams in challenging environments around the world, including conflict zones.

The Navy transformed Suzanne from a shy athletic student to being the tip of the spear, leading others in extraordinary and hair-raising situations. She joined the Navy as a raw 18-year-old small-town girl and left as a much-travelled and highly experienced U.S. Navy Captain, part of an elite group (the 1% of the 1% club) of women to reach this rank.

## THE TRANSITION

Suzanne left the US Navy at the start of 2022, after 26 years of service and shares this about her time there.

"The military set a strong foundation for who I am today and has helped me to become a sought-after professional speaker and expert advisor." She gained high caliber training and unbelievable experiences to develop insights and expertise that translate into solving real world problems effectively and efficiently. Her military training, experience, expertise, and mindset, "Have given me the jaw-dropping stories, the hard-won insights, and the high-level problem-solving skills to expertly advise business leaders and organizations." Her rolodex (what can we say, she's Gen X!) and a network of high-level contacts have also come in very handy for building out her professional profile.

Recently, she scaled up her advisory firm – Suzanne Lesko International – and used her global experiences as the foundation for her advisory. "I have branded myself as Xena, the Warrior Advisor™. 'Xena', my Navy call-sign; 'Warrior' to reflect my prior military background; and 'Advisor' to represent my new advisory career."

Suzanne has acted as a specialist advisor and subject matter expert to Grant Thornton, Valiant Integrated Services, and Wharton Leadership Ventures. Her first large-scale project was as a Federal Partner with Kyndryl (formerly IBM Global Services, the world's largest IT services company). "I helped them develop business development and go-to-market strategies for a new customer segment, the U.S. Federal sector." Suzanne recently joined Multiverse Health (MVH) – a start-up medical device manufacturer developing a compact, low-cost device that can detect lung cancer on a patient's breath in their doctor's office – as CEO. Her current MVH focus is on funding, strategy, and planning.

She also launched herself as a professional speaker, after undergoing intensive training with Heroic Public Speaking (HPS) in 2023. "Now, I have been shot at, captured and interrogated as a prisoner-of-war during training... but HPS is probably the most terrifying thing I have ever done!" Suzanne's keynote presentation is on the 'Amazing Adventures of the Warrior Advisor', whereby she uses her 'jaw-dropping tales of daring-do and daring-don't' to help audiences become more resilient and effective in business, life, and love.

Suzanne has also developed programs and workshops for her Resilient Leader Mindset™, and the Mastery of Optimal Performance philosophies. She is available as an advisor or leader for more complex engagements, such as start-up or non-profit management, public affairs consultancy, operations planning, and go-to-market strategies for companies.

## LESSONS LEARNED

Examine the situation quickly, pivot often, and make the most of every experience. As the character Forrest Gump once noted, "Life is like a box of chocolates. You never know what you're gonna get." As an example, Suzanne shares this story, "One time we are on a mission in Panama, and we need to urgently move to another vehicle. I'll leave it up to your imagination as to whether or not we were under fire from bad guys!!! We get to the van, climb in, realize it's a stick-shift... and no-one else knows how to drive one, except me. So, now I'm suddenly the designated driver for our flight crew, driving around a foreign country in a stick-shift van. I love that kind of stuff, and I thrive in those environments because I think that's where you learn your most."

## WHAT'S NEXT

Suzanne's main focus is on leading MVH to develop and launch its lifesaving device and increasing her professional speaking profile and engagements. She loves speaking with and advising client organizations, business leaders, high performance teams, and conference audiences with keynote presentations, panel participation, podcast guesting, workshops, and bespoke consulting projects.

Suzanne helps people transform their mindsets and, ultimately, their lives. "I help businesses and organizations level up and accelerate outcomes to become Resilient Leaders!"

## THE MILITARY EFFECT

On the positive side, Suzanne has also benefited greatly from the military. "I have a bachelor's degree in political science (with a minor in Spanish), and a master's degree in Global Leadership. I have senior military leadership experience, and expertise in operations planning and public affairs. Public affairs allowed me to work across all the sectors of the Navy, going where my talents matched the mission, and vice versa. I have also been exposed to, and learned to quickly understand, complex military and business projects."

# 43

## TAMEKA RUSHING, AIR FORCE

linkedin.com/in/tameka-rushing
**Hometown:** *Biloxi, Mississippi*
**Currently Resides:** *Arlington, Texas*

## WHY I SERVED

Born and raised by a single mom in Biloxi, Mississippi, Tameka and her brother, Taurian Murphy, spent much of their free time at the Boys and Girls Club. "The director was a retired Master Sergeant, Mr. Lee Kerley. He took us under his wing, sharing the importance of community service. He influenced my life and became like a father figure over the years." Growing up near an Air Force Base, Tameka knew she wanted to leave Mississippi, get an education, and see the world.

"My brother, 11 months older than me, decided to join the U.S. Air Force the year before I graduated high school. After joining, he said, 'You can do this too." Since Tameka looked up to her big brother, she said, "Okay!" She went to her brother's recruiter and signed up for the Air Force Delayed Enlistment Program.

Tameka's first military job was in supply chain management, where she spent 13 years. Her first assignment was at Osan Air Base, South Korea. While at her second assignment, Spangdahlem Air Base, Germany, Tameka became a mom to her son, Tarique Morales. She then moved on to Holloman Air Force Base, New Mexico. There, her family extended to include her daughter, Tionna Long. That is also where she was stationed when 9/11 happened. Tameka was responsible for preparing and executing teams' overseas deployments due to the conflict. From there, she moved her family and transitioned to Misawa Air Base, Japan, getting to work with more fighter jets. The following assignment was at Incirlik Air Base, Turkey. "Around this time, I met my first mentor, Senior Master Sergeant, Pamela Jones. She taught me so much about finding out what I wanted to be, who I wanted to become, and how I wanted to serve in and out of the Air Force." While stationed in Turkey, Tameka attended the Non-Commissioned Officer Academy in Germany. "By the time I ended that 6-week training course, I wanted to do this. I want to teach enlisted education. That started a fire."

Moving to Grand Forks Air Force Base, North Dakota, Tameka became aware of an opening to be the commandant of the Airman Leadership School. "The in-residence program equips Senior Airman to become proficient, first-time leaders capable of guiding and directing Air Force teams. I had only been on base for 4 months and didn't know many people." But the relationships she had proved to be huge, not only vouching for her but helping her secure the role. "Getting that job catapulted the rest of my career. I wasn't just the Commandant; I oversaw the faculty, the facility, the budget, the students, and the curriculum. I thank Brian Huber for believing in me and supporting me." Tameka finished her career at Barksdale Air Force Base, Louisiana, overseeing eight schools at eight different bases.

## THE TRANSITION

With her daughter in high school, Tameka was at a point in her life and career where she didn't want to move her again. "My son went to three high schools." It was also time for her to return to the Supply Chain Management career field. Not wanting to return to the supply chain side, she knew it was time. "I ended up retiring as Senior Master Sergeant (E-8), the same rank as my first mentor." Many of Tameka's mentors and peers were disappointed in her retirement decision. "I was one rank away from being in that top 1% of enlisted ranks (E-9). I walked away on my terms, having an amazing career, and living in four other countries. I took a leap of faith, like many women do at that stage in their career." Moving forward, she had no plan except to be a full-time mom for the first time. "That lasted all of two months," she joked.

New to the civilian world, Tameka applied for a local learning and development job. During the hiring process, she realized the hiring manager had prior military experience. "He had been in the Air Force, having worked at the Pentagon. He shared concerns regarding my master's degree not being complete. However, he understood military dynamics and knew my experience with enlisted education was unique." He went to bat for her. "Had it not been for his military experience and knowledge, I probably wouldn't have gotten the job."

Tameka's tenacity has continued to pay off. "Supported by my husband, I created my first business during COVID, partly because of a work furlough." Her venture, Eat the Lemons Apparel®, offers a unique collection of quirky, motivational t-shirts and more, some items catering specifically to veterans.

## LESSONS LEARNED

Being able to pivot, shift, and be adaptable is something that comes naturally for Tameka. "In most situations, I always ask myself, 'How can we fix it, make it right, and do what we need to do to be successful?'"

## WHAT'S NEXT

Launched in late '22, Glass Half Full Solutions LLC is Tameka's newest venture. "Essentially, we offer an experience that helps form inspirational leaders and unite teams. Our ideal client, including business owners, is the first time or emerging leader." The company's framework provides 1-on-1 coaching, group coaching, online learning, and workshops. Her goal is to pivot to a learning academy where all services have in-person and virtual options.

"I would love to do speaking engagements on pivoting and leadership, eventually writing a book on the subject. My whole life has been a pivot of good and bad: shifting assignments, job changes, new countries, relationships, children, etc."

Tameka is very active in the Greater Arlington Chamber of Commerce. "I joined the Veterans Business Council within the chamber and am an active resource for the Professional Development Committee. This council has become my biggest business advocate thus far. As an emerging business owner, I'm also integrating myself into other chamber councils. I've contributed to the chamber in a few ways, including a business resource blog highlighting leadership strategies shared on the chamber's LinkedIn and social media accounts."

## THE MILITARY EFFECT

"Reflecting on my life's journey through the lens of a veteran and a business owner, I've profoundly come to value diversity, mentorship, and community engagement. These experiences have shaped my professional ethos and deeply influenced my personal life, teaching me and my family the importance of embracing different cultures and serving others."

# 44

# TAMMY LAIRD, ARMY/AIR FORCE

linkedin.com/in/tammy-lynn-laird-32840816b
**Hometown:** *RAF Lakenheath & Arlington, Texas*
**Currently Resides:** *Granger, Texas*

## WHY I SERVED

"My father was in the Air Force, so I grew up in it. I just loved the military environment, knowing we were serving a purpose bigger than ourselves and serving our country. The whole family was somewhat involved." Wanting to follow in her father's footsteps, Tammy met with an Air Force recruiter while in high school. She was impressed more with her Army recruiter. "For some reason, God had other plans. I have been able to reach more people for being both Army and Air Force."

Going into the Army, Tammy met people from all walks of life. "When I went to boot camp, I observed much...there were people from all walks of life, southern, northern, etc. That was very eye-opening to those who grew up isolated from others. We were trained well by the Drill Sergeants because all of a sudden, we weren't Black, White, Asian, Hispanic, Purple, etc. We were all green and we all bled red, no rhyme intended. It was amazing to see those human interactions and then the camaraderie and the friendships that developed from that. The ideal environment to be curious about others and to learn from everyone. If you think about it, that is what makes America the best of many worlds blended together. Creative gifts and talents and brilliant ideas unified to defend and uphold freedom."

## THE TRANSITION

As Tammy exited the military, she had no idea how painful the transition would be. It would take 7 years before she felt normal again. She missed her brothers and sisters so much on occasion, it was hard to breathe. But having done everything she wanted to do in the Air Force, Tammy's career ended on a voluntary separation. "My husband and I had our first son. And I just didn't want the daycare raising him. My birthday present to him when he turned 1 years old was to not leave him again."

As she slowly reentered the workforce, Tammy would only take jobs where her son could come with her. This included daycare positions and later substitute teaching preschool classes. "We began homeschooling shortly thereafter, working independently, and later with other families and cooperatives. Within the last 3 years, we became part of a new homeschool community, coming alongside families called Classical Conversations." This organization follows the classical education method and helps children to learn how to think, not what to think. "It's been awesome because no matter where families go, the curriculum is the same. We see a lot of military families and it has brought me much comfort to know my children are learning with military brats, the same way I grew up. It's an awesome way to meet people who have experienced friendships from all over the world."

Tammy also began to embrace writing. "I have always been a writer. My second book is called *Valiant Charlie Defeats the Sleep Monster*. It's a progressive story about obstructive sleep apnea and sleep disordered breathing in children, and the importance of catching it early to make a significant change for good in a child's life. Writing for a purpose to help educate and help others heal is a passion, and I am grateful it has and is making a difference in the lives of children."

Within the last 3.5 years, she became part of a military family once more through the LinkedIn network. It started with Angels14, a weekly Zoom comprised of military members from all branches and in all phases and civilian allies. "We would just meet for camaraderie, connection, and community. This led to a connection with 22ZERO." Not only was Tammy healed from much trauma, she has also been able to join their mission and help heal over 250 veterans, first responders, their families and Gold Star Family members.

## LESSONS LEARNED

If it matters to you, it matters. There is no need to compare yourself to anyone else.

## WHAT'S NEXT

A firm believer that God wastes nothing, she has been able to see His hand guiding her along life's paths. Her many experiences from the Army, Air Force, post military, and every level of school from preschool through college has given Tammy plenty of words to create new stories that capture life's joys and challenges. Her next project is a book to be called Healing Heroes. "It's for our first responders, including military and their families. Stuffed animals are telling the story." Her book is being written to shed light on the behind the scenes of what first responders may go through. "I have firefighters, police officers, and military in there. We also have foreign service officers and civilian contractors that experience much as they deploy with our military too."

Not an original fan of social media, Tammy utilizes it only when necessary but has found it invaluable. "In my work with 22ZERO (https://22zero. org/), I am amazed at how close I am with those I work with on a daily basis, some I have never even met in person. For some, I'm closer to them than I am to people I see every day." For her, there is no greater joy than to see another brother or sister healed.

## THE MILITARY EFFECT

"Thanks to 22ZERO, I can now help veterans and first responders without knowing their stories through the processes executed. Thankfully, my clients do not share their traumas, so they are not reliving anything either. Finally, a solution to heal our brothers and sisters. Knowing, they can be healed fills my heart with so much joy!"

## 45

# TRACEY JONES, AIR FORCE

linkedin.com/in/drtraceycjones
**Hometown:** *Camp Hill, Pennsylvania*
**Currently Resides:** *Enola, Pennsylvania*

## WHY I SERVED

Upon graduating high school, Tracey was at a crossroads, uncertain about her path. Her father, a staunch patriot, delivered an inspiring leadership speech at the New Mexico Military Institute (NMMI) in Roswell, NM. Upon his return, he placed a pamphlet about the institute in front of her, describing the program and imparting a valuable lesson: "In life, you must always earn your stripes. The students at NMMI are destined to achieve greatness." Tracey fondly remembers her father as a dynamic and ethical businessman who emphasized the unwavering character of military personnel. His words ignited a fire within her, prompting her to say, "I aspire to possess that utmost character. I want to make a significant impact on my life."

Tracey obtained her associate degree from NMMI. While many of her peers pursued paths to West Point, she became aware of a groundbreaking military institution, the United States Air Force Academy in Colorado, which began admitting women in 1980. She attributes her successful admission to Major John Schaeffer, her liaison officer, who played a pivotal role in securing her place at the Air Force Academy. This opportunity was a catalyst that kept her focused and moving forward, leading her to affirm, "Saying 'yes' to that opportunity remains one of the best decisions I ever made."

Upon graduation, Tracey embarked on a distinguished career as a fighter aircraft maintenance officer, overseeing various critical aspects, from crew chiefs and avionics technicians to weapons handlers. Her initial assignment at Shaw AFB in SC took her to Operation DESERT SHIELD/STORM, and she later transferred to USAFE, where she actively participated in the Bosnian War.

## THE TRANSITION

After an illustrious twelve-year military career, Tracey faced a pivotal moment. Despite initial uncertainty, her entrepreneurial spirit prevailed, and she adeptly leveraged her military experience to transition into civilian life. Attending a hiring fair, Tracey encountered numerous organizations dedicated to placing former military personnel in roles that align with their skills and experiences. She was pleasantly surprised to receive nearly twenty job offers, a realization of the transferability and relevance of her honed operational skills acquired on the flight line and in logistics.

Tracey launched into the high-volume semiconductor industry, serving as a project manager for Applied Materials. She then ventured into the defense sector with Northrop Grumman's Space Technology Division before running a large, diverse Base Operations Service Contract (BOSC) for the National Security Agency (NGA West).

In 2009, Tracey assumed leadership at Tremendous Leadership, a company founded by her father in 1967. She proudly remarks, "We have fostered collaborations with distinguished authors such as Jim Stoval, Mark Sanborn, Ken Blanchard, Don Hutson, and Brian Tracy, among others. Our mission is to publish transformative material, one book at a time, to influence positive change in the world."

Tracey's lifelong ambition included earning a Ph.D. In 2015, she began her academic journey, focusing on crisis leadership and follower self-efficacy. Simultaneously, she ventured into public speaking, recognizing that most of her audience held terminal degrees. Her involvement as a trustee at Lancaster Bible College led to her enrollment in their Ph.D. program, culminating in her degree attainment in 2019.

In 2018, Tracey was invited by her contacts in the life insurance industry to join the advisory council for The Center for Military and Veterans Affairs at The American College. This organization facilitates the transition of military personnel, their spouses, and disabled veterans to lucrative careers within the financial services sector. Last year, she assumed the esteemed role of Chairperson.

With an impressive literary portfolio of twelve books, five tailored for children, Tracey fondly recalls the inspiration behind her maiden book—a rescue dog named Mister Blue, adopted while working in Austin.

## LESSONS LEARNED

Grow your experience bag; every new experience gives you another key.

## WHAT'S NEXT

Presently, Tracey's time revolves around teaching leadership, executive coaching, and sharing the transformative power of books. She recently assumed the role of Adjunct Professor at the American College of Financial Services, where she guides financial professionals on their journey to earning the prestigious Chartered Leadership Fellow® (CLF®) designation. This program equips professionals with the foresight and leadership acumen required to facilitate their organization's growth in alignment with strategic objectives.

Her current focus centers on the podcast "Tremendous Leadership" and her newsletter. These ventures took flight during the pandemic, serving as platforms to disseminate positivity and inspiration. She continues to generate engaging content, encouraging individuals to follow these channels for the latest updates. Tracey recently celebrated the landmark of her 150th podcast episode, where she engages in enlightening conversations with leaders from diverse backgrounds and career stages, delving into the sacrifices and prerequisites of leadership.

Additionally, Tracey remains actively engaged in several boards affiliated with educational initiatives in emerging countries. She still oversees the operations of her publishing company's warehouse, taking a hands-on approach. Personally, signing books and adding thoughtful notes has become integral to her commitment to her readers.

Tracey eloquently encapsulates her philosophy: "Life, in its essence, combines the elements of poetry and plumbing. The endless blue skies are inspiring, but a well-thought-out blueprint is indispensable. My mission is to uncover the threads that bind us all and discover the universal truths of leadership."

## THE MILITARY EFFECT

Tracey reflects on the profound impact of her military service, acknowledging its enduring significance by stating, "Those twelve years continue to open doors beyond imagination. I am profoundly proud and deeply grateful for the privilege of serving this great nation alongside my brothers and sisters in arms." She attributes the military to setting a clear vision and mission for her life, propelling her towards excellence.

# 46

## TRAVIS MILLS, ARMY

linkedin.com/in/ssgtravismills
**Hometown:** *Vassar, Michigan*
**Currently Resides:** *Manchester, Maine*

## WHY I SERVED

A redshirt freshman playing college football, Travis was having a hard time focusing on academics. "I was always walking by the recruiting table and thought about my dad who was in the Army. It seemed like the best thing to do." Not one to waste time, or money, he signed up.

"My uncle always said to like the work I do for the military and make sure it works for me." Travis was a Band of Brothers fan, and then saw a video of the Airborne Infantry. "Let's do that!", he said. And two weeks later he shipped out.

## THE TRANSITION

"I always planned on doing 20 years, become an officer and be a black hat at Fort Bragg." Travis had a goal to retire as a Major, be a high school teacher and football coach, and own a landscape company in the summer. But all that changed in an instant.

After his injury, Travis was sent to Walter Reed. "I always enjoyed being a role model and was quickly cast into that position." He remembers when a private in his platoon was nearby in wound care in tears. "As a staff sergeant, I was often looked up to. This soldier needed my support, and I made sure to be by his side".

While still going through rehab, Travis was contacted by a group who wanted to do a documentary on him. "During this time one of my friends saw my drive to give back and serve others. They encouraged me to get out there and tell my story." He soon became a public speaker and started The Travis Mills Foundation.

The first speaking engagement was a memorable one. Says Travis, "I was at a science convention talking about STEM, and my time slot was against Bill Nye the Science Guy. Everyone had to walk past me to get to Bill, but they stopped and listened to my presentation instead."

In 2014, Travis moved to Maine so his wife could be closer to her family. "The Gary Sinese Foundation built me a smart home (along with Tunnels for Tower & Caring Charitable Foundation)." He started flipping houses and soon bought a marina. "Two years ago, we opened a restaurant."

The Travis Mills Foundation now has 35 employees and a budget of $4.5 million dollars. Traveling 150 days a year to speak, he handed the reins to Heather Hempill who is now the Executive Director. "Everyone who works for me is like an extended family." That being said, even his parents come up for 5 months each summer to help out at the marina.

## LESSONS LEARNED

You get one go around to make the most of life.

## WHAT'S NEXT

"I'm not scared to try anything, even though I'm much softer as a civilian". These days, his bread and butter come from public speaking. "The businesses are set for the long term, and I take no income from The Travis Mills Foundation."

His biggest driver is his children. Says Travis, "I don't want them to feel like they are missing out because dad's a robot. I'm very involved in the community, and well known as a father, a philanthropist, and an entrepreneur."

With a never quit attitude, the restaurant will soon expand to include a brewery and distillery. Travis also just started a clothing line and has a few other endeavors he's working on. "My only job is to give purpose and direction. I'll never dwell on the past, it's not something I can control."

Always focused on helping others, Travis loves to post videos on Instagram and share the success of those around him. "I love to find ways to help people achieve successes." With this constant drive he also focuses on growing the Foundation. "Every year we will increase our donations, increase our size, and increase the offerings." They have focused on growth of the program focused on PTSD with the Warrior Path Foundation. Travis hopes to expand and add a new facility making the program 24-weeks long.

So what else can Travis hope to accomplish? "I wouldn't mind doing a reality TV show and a motion picture movie. There is a high demand and it's time to share more."

## THE MILITARY EFFECT

"A veteran will always get the job done, no matter what time of day. We were responsible for people's lives; we can certainly be responsible for most any job required."

# 47

## TYLER VAN HOOK, MARINES

linkedin.com/in/tylervanhook
**Hometown:** *Nokesville, Virginia*
**Currently Resides:** *Southern Shores, North Carolina*

## WHY I SERVED

Tyler grew up modestly with his parents and two brothers in a small country town on the outskirts of Washington D.C. Growing up he faced some challenging life events which led him to acting out and getting into small trouble here and there. During his high school years, he recognized he was following a trajectory that was unsustainable and fell short of the role model he aspired to be for his younger brothers. Tyler attended an alternative school in Northern Virginia, comprised of students from rough backgrounds. "It was like pretty much all of the troubled kids that were brought into some very bad circumstances into one school. We had to have a security guard in each one of our classrooms."

Alternative schools present an excellent opportunity for military recruiters to connect with students, offering them a chance to transform their lives and make a meaningful contribution to their country. One day, Tyler and his friends encountered a Marine recruiter, which presented a great opportunity to get his life back on track and be the person he wanted to be for himself and his family. "His name was Sergeant Sol, and he literally looked like he would take someone's soul. Just back from Iraq, he was very imposing with tattoos and a commanding personality. Then he called us all punks and challenged everyone to do a pull up. Being from the middle of nowhere, I knew he could back it up. It became a goal of mine to prove to him I could do ten."

For Tyler, it was that "right place, right time" that gave him the rudder he needed to change the course of his life. "I practiced anywhere I could to do pull ups, sit ups, and run and then went to the Marine office ready to retest." The Sergeant was impressed, challenging Tyler to put his money where his mouth was and sign up. "It was a challenge getting in. I needed to have all state requirements completed for my high school diploma and got it in two months. Sergeant Sol would call me every day making sure I studied." Immediately after achieving all the requirements, Tyler was off to Paris Island at the age of 17.

Living in Okinawa, Japan at the age of eighteen, Tyler entered the reconnaissance community. "I wanted to be the best reconnaissance Marine that I could be. From 17 to 28 I deployed mostly every year. So, I would party for thirty days, deploy, come back, party for thirty days do the work up, deploy again. That was my 20's." For Tyler, the most difficult time of his career was still to come.

"I was the Chief Instructor at the Marine Raider Training Center. My sole mission in life was to assess junior Marines' suitability and train them to become Special Operations. I developed and assessed them, and at the end of the day made a recommendation on whether they should continue, be dropped, or recycled to the next class. That was probably the most difficult time in my entire military career and probably the most heavily weighed on me." He created a new process to find the best operators. "I thought that the process that we were doing was archaic and the team and I engineered a new way to do it, which allowed us to increase the throughput while increasing the standard which is not common."

## THE TRANSITION

"I was out in Iraq in 2021. Coming back from that deployment, I realized that my operational time had come to an end." Back in his life was Colleen, a woman he had known since being a young child. "We grew up on opposite sides of the train tracks so to speak and stayed in touch all those years, but nothing ever materialized romantically."

Over the years, Tyler & Colleen would meet, go out on a date, and then go their separate ways. "It was like a Dirk's Bentley song. I saw taillights leaving the bar." But then, in between a deployment they reconnected. "She came to visit me down at Camp Lejeune, and we've been together ever since."

Tyler was officially retired and felt like he was in a mid-life crisis from a loss of a sense of purpose. "I didn't take care of myself and felt like I was riding a coffin about halfway through my deployments. I'd seen some of the best guys in the military that I've ever seen walk this earth pass away. I kind of adopted this mindset of when it's time for your ticket to get punched, it's going to get punched." Colleen told him things had to change. "She was the ultimate sounding board and helped me navigate through dark times. Colleen helped us pioneer a way to leverage resources dedicated to service members." Ultimately, Tyler went to Warriors Heart (https://www.warriorsheart.com/). "It ignited this huge soul-searching journey for myself, and I started taking a lot of ownership. Discipline in the military and of yourself are two very different things."

"When I got out, I decided to do some consulting." Tyler adds, "I was consulting for a government entity, and they asked me to look at their training pipeline for federal agents and officers." While there, he realized that the issues they were trying to solve were the same as at Marsoc (https://www.marsoc.marines.mil/) where Tyler served. It was the start of a new journey, and Kognitiv Edge (https://www.kognitivedge.com/) was created, which is where we digitally transform the way elite team train and operate.

## LESSONS LEARNED

Know what your strengths are. Know what your weaknesses are play to your hand but in the background you hyper focused on what's lacking. Strive daily to improve.

## WHAT'S NEXT

Kognitive Edge was recently launched by Tyler and his wife. "This is for the most important people in the world, our military." With focus on delivering solutions, he continues to surround himself with the best and brightest minds. "I recently applied to and been accepted at Brown University. Its program allows you to work on your business."

The company's first mission is state and local law enforcement. Says Tyler, "From a business perspective, it's hard to do because of budgets. But if I can prove myself with the most elite organizations in the world, I can then lobby Congress to get the funding that they need. this will allow us to run these individuals through psychological evaluations, establish baselines for them, and make sure they get the appropriate training needed."

Looking ahead, Kognitive Edge also hopes to work in the commercial space, specifically with underprivileged athletes. There are also plans to open a Rehab facility or some type of facility that brings in people who want to legitimately make a difference. If you can take individuals in the gutter and put them back on the playing field and have them be a productive member of society, that's winning. You gotta pay it forward."

## THE MILITARY EFFECT

"What other job do you get the passion for and what other service could you provide to the world as much as defending its freedom? I think that that's hard to understand and realize that you're not that anymore. You're not who you were in uniform. But what you can be is a positive disruptor and you have to figure out where that is."

# 48

## VALERIE LAVIN, ARMY

linkedin.com/in/valerieellis7
**Hometown:** *Sunrise Beach, Missouri*
**Currently Resides:** *St. Pete, Florida*

## WHY I SERVED

Though Valerie's father served in Vietnam, she never intended to join the military. Valerie had her sights set on college immediately after high school. After completing her freshman year she decided to sit out the next semester to save money and transfer to a state college. "A friend needed a roommate and asked me to come back to Bolivar, Missouri to live with her. So, I picked up my waitressing at the Western Sizzlin' and moved back."

One night after work she was sitting on the couch eating Domino's pizza. Said Valerie, "I remember every detail, what kind of pizza I was eating, and even the living room. So, I'm sitting there watching Private Benjamin starring Goldie Hawn, and decide at that point to join the Army." Knowing the movie wasn't a true representation of what she would experience, Valerie still felt that something about it resonated with her, probably because her father served, and she was raised with similar military discipline coupled with mid-western values. "I called my dad the next day and he helped me talk with the recruiter."

"I enlisted as a Signal and non-Morse Code Interceptor Analyst." Valerie went to basic training at Fort Jackson, South Carolina and then got her orders for Morse Code School at Ft Devens, MA. From there, she went to Corry Station in Pensacola to get trained as a Cryptologist. "When I was assigned to my first duty station, I was the only Signals Intelligence Analyst in the entire brigade. The rest of the Battalion's mission was counterintelligence and human intelligence." Thankfully, the Director of her division was a retired Signal Intelligence Warrant Officer who taught her not only how to be a SIGINT analyst, but also a leader. She still carries many of those leadership lessons with her today.

Soon after her second enlistment, Valerie knew she would make the Army a career. "It was my intent to complete my 20-year career then use my G.I. Bill to finish college. When 9/11 happened, Valerie noticed many struggling with not only the attack, but why they joined the military. Was it simply for the G.I. Bill, to leave what was troubling back home or was it truly for God and Country? She witnessed it as a decision point for many. For Valerie, there was no doubt. "Sometimes, you don't realize your commitment to something until it's challenged. My parents understood and appreciated the luxury we have in being Americans and they instilled that in me and my siblings. Looking back that's probably why, while devastated by the attack and the loss of American lives, I wasn't scared to continue to serve and do my part in the fight."

## THE TRANSITION

"I had no idea that veterans struggled with employment. But it was a hot topic when I retired in 2014." Says Valerie, "I'm in this room full of peers transitioning a various ranks and lengths of service, hearing the worry in their voice about how to navigate the next steps and as I'm integrating into the veteran community, I'm meeting veterans that have been unemployed for 12, 18, even 24 months. And these are not just junior enlisted. There were some Sergeant Majors and Colonels. I couldn't believe it. Often, we would hear 'retiring as a Sergeant First Class is respectable. You won't have any problems finding a job, they will want to hire you for your experience and leadership skills. I drank that Kool-Aid too, but after retiring it dawned on me those saying that were senior leaders that were still serving so how did they know?"

Dating her soon-to-be husband, Valerie knew that his recruiting firm was always looking for qualified candidates. "He was a recruiter whose role was to staff CFOs and accountants across all industries." Spending over two decades in the military, Valerie was fascinated to learn about his work and the business landscape. "I didn't know anything other than military jobs and I'd never dated a civilian before. He was teaching me all kinds of things about business and how employers select employees."

Valerie's initial plan was to go to school and be a physical therapist with a focus on geriatrics. "After talking with my husband and friends, I put school on the back burner so I could figure out how to help veterans get employment." Her first experience was with a veteran owned business. "I was hired on the spot and didn't even have to show my resume which I had paid $300 to have an expert help me write. The owner said, "As a retired Army First Sergeant, I know what you're capable of."

Realizing the job role wasn't fulfilling enough as she felt like she could help so many more Veterans find not just jobs, but careers they qualified for, so she started her own veteran staffing company. "I made the move through encouragement from a mentor. She was a highly successful executive in the industry. I was often asked to help find veterans for jobs, and how to understand veteran resumes. Plus, with my mentor and my husband's experience I had the support system to help me learn and navigate the hiring process to help."

"I probably spent as much money on coffee as I made in retirement the first year that my company was open, because I thought that's what you did when you're trying to build this, right?" Valerie would have coffee with everybody. "Through these conversations I wanted to demonstrate

I was experienced enough to help them find the right veteran for their open positions." She continues, "It failed miserably for many reasons. As a company helping transitioning veterans, I had to compete with free services offered to employees, and also had to fight against the stigmatization of hiring veterans such as PTSD."

While running her staffing company, Valerie got a call from a local community college that had gotten a grant for veteran entrepreneurship. "My last position at MacDill Air Force Base was the Commandant Headquarters' First Sergeant coupled with running my business, I had become very recognizable as a military and veteran advocate in the community, and I had quite a network." She was asked to be program manager for their entrepreneurship program for the community college. "That's where I got my first exposure to the entrepreneurial ecosystem in Tampa. I completely fell in love with this space. The ecosystem even in 2015 was so rich of resources and support. I took great pride in supporting these aspiring entrepreneurs to realize their dream of small business ownership. I poured my soul into this mission which would lead to the launch of a nonprofit."

## LESSONS LEARNED

Keep learning. It's part of the military culture to constant training in leadership and technical skills. Continuing with this mentality will help you continue to evolve as you discover who you are beyond combat boots and camouflage.

## WHAT'S NEXT

In June of 2016 I launched Luminary Global. My husband left his staffing firm early in 2017 to join me in building the company. In 2019, we were forced to pivot quickly. We started to make phone calls looking for opportunities to sell products." Selling products was always part of the vision to complement their services but it happened much quicker than planned. "The first opportunity we landed on was a Tactical Medical supply order. Despite the challenges and the accelerated timeline, we couldn't have landed in a better spot. Luminary allows me and my husband to use our natural and learned talents to solve problems for our customers. It was hell getting here and we're still dealing with past challenges. But everything happens for a reason, and eight years later we are still here! Our country was built on the backs of entrepreneurs, and I'm privileged to be part of America's fabric as a small business owner.

We were recently approached by an Action Zone Alumni to start another company with two of his former Green Beret team members." The offer of this opportunity was a surprise. Says Valerie, "Their recognition of our ability and expertise validated that all the hardships and challenges we've been through with Luminary was worth it. Despite our previous unpleasant experiences in the past, we are looking forward to this partnership and growing the company with fellow veterans.

## THE MILITARY EFFECT

In 2018 Valerie, along with a few other entrepreneurs, a military spouse and two veterans, launched Action Zone. "It is a nonprofit that provides education and training to veterans, military spouses, and their adult children to start, build and grow their businesses." In creating the business model, the founders knew they didn't want to host networking events due to their manpower constraints. "I had known about Bunker Labs(https://bunkerlabs.org/) and their networking events they called Bunker Brews. I was introduced to one of the Regional Directors so I could ask them to launch a chapter in Tampa. This would allow us to teach about entrepreneurship and they could bring the veteran community together through Bunker Brews. They asked me to become the Inaugural city leader which I gladly agreed." With the collaborative relationship between Action Zone and Bunker labs the veteran entrepreneur community scaled in Tampa.

## 49

## VIAN MORALES, ARMY

linkedin.com/in/vian-b-morales
**Hometown:** *Macon, Georgia*
**Currently Resides:** *Savannah, Georgia*

## WHY I SERVED

Coming from a family with a deep commitment to military service, Vian always felt alignment with a military career path. "My Grandfather, SSgt Burnes C. Brown served in the Rome-Arno Campaign and Po Valley during WWII, my dad, Spc Kenneth R. Brown was drafted and served in South Korea, one brother, MSgt Ronald Brown, served in many campaigns, and another brother, Commander Burnes C. Brown just took command of the USS South Dakota. It was our family norm and for all of us a commitment of service."

Not one to take a traditional path solely focused on the military, her competitive spirit and passion for sports fueled her aspirations to play soccer in college. Preparing for the next level she was contacted by the Citadel. "I had no clue who they were, but my mom did. Her friends thought she was nuts to encourage me to even entertain the idea!" Women had only been admitted a few years before and the road wasn't as easy one.

"In good ole Citadel fashion, when recruiting athletes, my campus visit started on a Friday afternoon. The precision and discipline of the cadets at Friday parade was impressive, then everyone took off on leave. The campus just looked beautiful, the team was kind and I thought I could make an impact, it all seemed doable." She prepped and read all the books about The Citadel, trained even harder but as she says, "Nothing fully prepares you." "When I showed up for Hell Week, I got my hair cut by 'Shaky Willy', a sweet barber at the Citadel for over many years, you can assume the reason behind the nickname. I'll just say the goal of those haircuts wasn't for us to look great and I sure didn't come out looking like Halle Berry."

On campus, Vian caught on quickly and learned how to balance the life of a student-athlete, early morning weight training and PT, long days in the classroom and on the field, and late nights studying and shining shoes and belt buckles. Her interest in joining the military became stronger in her sophomore year. "I was really interested in joining the Air Force but with my history of childhood asthma, even as a Division I athlete with no complications, that door shut quickly. She graduated as the 33rd Black Female graduate. But 9/11 was constantly on her mind. "I wanted to do more. So, I decided while I got my master's at Georgia State, I would commission through their ROTC program."

"I was drawn to the camaraderie, the level of discipline that was ingrained in me from an early age and the resilience of a mission first mindset. Most importantly, I was incredibly lucky to find mentors who guided and supported my career providing me the opportunity to work at the command level on special projects at USARC and USACAPOC at Ft. Bragg, NC quite early in my career and at many other quality organizations that created space for growth thereafter." Vian hung up her boots after her last assignment as the Detachment Commander of the 188th Infantry Brigade out of Ft. Stewart, Ga.

## THE TRANSITION

"My husband and I were doing our best to sustain life as a dual military family, but things just became too out of balance." With her husband's last deployment and a young daughter, Vian didn't know if they could pull it off with a growing family much longer. "I just felt off kilter. I quickly recognized the burnout and mental health issues surrounding me. If I'm honest, looking back there were more people than not struggling alongside me. We just didn't talk about it." She felt with her skill set that she could do even more outside the military and have a better work-life balance. "I knew I could serve the world in a better way. I could show up for the people around me better than I could have if I stayed in. I wasn't completely sure what direction I wanted to go in, but I knew I could take a military operational mind and just shift it into a business one." She tapped into her network, stayed consistent and patient, and was quickly noticed by a military program recruiting for Dell, where Vian then moved onto various government and business consulting roles.

Through tragedy and deep work, she settled into her roles and re-grounded herself through yoga, meditation, breath work, and sound healing, making it her mission to use her skillset to bring holistic practices to others. "I am particularly passionate about making holistic health more accessible to veterans and those who suffer from chronic conditions. I watched friends suffer and we all felt like there was nowhere to turn to. If we only save one life, that's enough for me but I certainly believe we can do so much more."

## LESSONS LEARNED

"One thing that the military doesn't do the best job at is instilling in us is the power of human connection and asking for help. Embrace the power of human connection. Our communities are our greatest assets. We are our own mycelium. Engage with your network, let them know what you are looking for and ask them what they are looking for."

## WHAT'S NEXT

Vian is now the SVP of Operations at Beckley Retreats. "We offer a comprehensive 11-week program rooted in the power of psychedelics, mindfulness, and community. Our multidisciplinary model empowers our participants to develop the mindset, knowledge and skills to promote personal discovery and holistic wellbeing across body, mind, heart, and spirit."

She recently held a program sponsoring eleven combat veterans with traumatic brain injuries in partnership with Imperial College London and the Heroic Hearts Project studying the benefits of psychedelic-assisted therapies in combatting the veteran suicide epidemic among service members. Vian says, one veteran shared, "I always knew the definition of compassion, but I never understood or felt compassion for myself or anyone until this experience. This retreat was a lifetime of therapy worth of healing."

In 2024, she hopes to raise $500,000 for The Beckley Retreat Scholarship Fund. "We want to be able to sponsor one-hundred people to attend our programs. Imagine a world where communities are no longer burdened by the weight of generational trauma and discrimination, where veterans are supported and held as they heal the wounds of their service to our country." Vian continues, "We must create opportunities for underserved, underrepresented and underprivileged communities. Everyone should have access to alternative modalities for health and well-being. There's just a lack of information and access in our communities that's unacceptable. But with support, I'm hopeful we'll get there."

## THE MILITARY EFFECT

"I think there is a level of appreciation in all workforces for service members and their skill set. There's also this imbalance in understanding what military people have done and what can relate to this other side of the world. It's important we bridge those gaps when we are in a position to do so. Service members often undervalue themselves because you might not see all of the underlying things that you've really been trained to do, but you can knock these other jobs out of the park. It's just about switching systems. You're just stepping into a different colored room, but you still know how to paint the room. It's almost perception versus reality, isn't it?"

# 50

## VICTORIA RYDIN BONCZ, AIR FORCE

linkedin.com/in/victoria-rydin-boncz
**Hometown:** *Ingleside, Illinois*
**Currently Resides:** *Navarre, Florida*

## WHY I SERVED

A small-town girl from Northern Illinois, Victoria grew up in a working-class family. "No one in my family had been to college and I just didn't see it as much of an option." Watching her friends apply, she was lost. "I just knew I didn't want to stay in this town. I needed a way out; a way to make something of myself."

Knowing very little about the military, most of her assumptions were from movies. Her father served in the Navy but didn't speak of it much. The guy Victoria was dating in high school joined the Marines, but she knew that was way too hard-core for her. She wanted to know more about the Army and Air Force to figure out which one would be a better fit.

Victoria's parents didn't go with her to the recruiter. "All the recruiters are in the same office area and the Army always tries to suck you in first. I learned about the Reserves from them. Then I went to the Air Force recruiter and found out there wasn't a reserve option, which I found out later that wasn't true." The recruiter showed her the dorm layout and touted the quality of life and how it was so much better than the Army. "I was sold." She went home and told her parents the decision. She was a junior when she signed up for the delayed enlistment program.

Entering the Air Force very soon after graduation, Victoria planned to do four years and then head to college. Not thinking long-term about choosing a career, she chose her career field based on what she thought would be exciting and fun. Having only flown once in her life, Victoria joked that she just selected her job because she "wanted to touch planes." Her Dad was a general contractor, and she often went to job sights with him, learning from him. "When it came to the entry exam, my highest score was maintenance, so that's where I started." Assigned to survival equipment, she was soon packing parachutes and working on ejection seats. "It became mind-numbing for me. I loved the camaraderie in the squadron, but I knew exactly what I was doing every single day I went to work. There was no challenge to it, except physical." She started to look for other options.

In '99, Victoria went on deployment to Kuwait. During the welcome briefing, a non-commissioned officer from public affairs officer talked to the group about various rules and programs for the location. "I raised my hand and basically told him I want your job; how do I do that. A bit caught off guard, he said, "Well, you can come to work for me. I worked nights in my survival equipment job, then went to Public Affairs and learned from him. He is still my mentor and a good friend." What started out as a four-year goal, turned into a 26-year career.

## THE TRANSITION

Victoria's decision to conclude her career was a roller coaster of emotions. She was working at AFSOC (Air Force Special Operations Command), and I loved it. "I finally felt like I was at home and where I belonged." When she was next in line for a move to a new base, the decision had to be made. "AFSOC was home. I also recently had family move in with us. My husband loved it here. I couldn't imagine moving. It was time."

It was a leap of faith. "I did my calculations on the military retirement calculator and figured out I was okay." She knew her skills would probably transfer over to a great job, especially if she used her extensive network of retired Public Affairs friends and former colleagues. But she knew she needed to take a break, needed to take some time to herself.

"I'm still in that transition phase. It's been about a year." Victoria was so burnt out that the first job she even considered was pet sitting. "I needed a break and didn't want to use my brain in any capacity, except for just to figure things out. Figure out who I was and what I truly wanted in this next chapter."

Like all veterans, she went through TAPS (a mandatory course to learn about benefits, how to write a resume, etc.). Victoria reached out to resource groups like, Hiring our Heroes(www.hiringourheroes.org), (Four Block(https://fourblock.org/), and The Honor Foundation(https://www.honor.org/).

## LESSONS LEARNED

You can learn something from every single person you encounter. Never discount someone else's experiences.

## WHAT'S NEXT

Always interested in real estate, Victoria and her husband bought their first investment condo in the Florida panhandle. "We have always had long-term rentals, but this is our first vacation rental. I love talking to our guests and trying to make sure they have the best trip specific to their needs. We are also looking at expanding, just don't know where yet."

She also teaches leadership & personal development online. "I'm now contracted to teach once or twice a month. It happened totally by chance through my network, leading to the opportunity. Like I said, everything works out." Victoria has an additional project in crisis communication, and a PR firm that sends her collaboration work. She also has several four-legged clients and has built quite a pet care business.

"I just think that I'm an intuitive and super adaptable problem solver. And I've just figured out how to talk to people, how to communicate and figure out what they need and deliver. And I've always been known as the one that is going to tell you what you need to hear, even if it is a bit harsh. Most people appreciate it, once they get used to it." Victoria loves the freedom to make her own schedule. "I can take on clients if I want to." With her father battling dementia, the focus has shifted. "He's my number one priority. My schedule revolves around that commitment to my family, and I am super grateful I have that flexibility."

## THE MILITARY EFFECT

"There are thousands of organizations that want to see Veterans succeed. I didn't know this until I was retiring, and I wish I knew it earlier. There are so many people out there that are ready to help us, but we shouldn't wait until we are a year out from retirement. It is a huge transition after being told where to live, what to do, and what to wear. It has been mission, mission, mission for years and now we have to think about ourselves."

# BIOGRAPHIES

**APRIL SHPRINTZ** was named one of the Top 22 Entrepreneurs of 2023 by New York Weekly, she is a Business Accelerator & Leading Sales Expert helping entrepreneurs and companies make huge increases in revenue while working less using the principles of The Generosity Culture®.

April has spent more than 25 years in multiple industries solving problems, driving growth, and accelerating companies. Generating over $1.2 Billion dollars in direct revenue using the principles of The Generosity Culture®, April has helped entrepreneurs go from no revenue to closing $100K deals week after week in a month, taken failing companies to profitability in less than six months, and scaled multimillion dollar international firms to 8 figures in less than a year.

A proud veteran, April served for nearly 7 years in the Air Force where she was a Television News Anchor and Executive Producer of AFTV News with an audience of 75 million. Today, April hosts a Global Top 10 Ranking "how to" podcast called "Winning Mindset Mastery", sharing her learnings and processes to develop a winning mindset for success in life and business. April is the author of the Award Winning "Magic Blue Rocks, The Secret To Doing Anything," and has been featured in Forbes, Newsweek and Thrive Global as well as on CBS, NBC, ABC and Fox Sports.

**BLAKE HOGAN** served as an Officer in the Marine Corps from 2008-2012. Following his service in the Marines, he helped develop markets for Sage Glass, a green tech construction product that was later acquired by Saint Gobain.

With nearly ten years of experience as a veteran entrepreneur and leader, Blake is passionate about empowering fellow veterans and their spouses to start and scale successful businesses. He recently led the successful acquisition of Bunker Labs by Syracuse University's D'Aniello Institute of Veterans and Military Families where together; they can create a "Center of Gravity" for veteran and military spouse entrepreneurship. Prior to the acquisition, Blake served as CEO of Bunker Labs, a national nonprofit organization he oversaw the strategic vision, operations, and partnerships of a network growing from 20 to 40 chapters across the country, serving more than 4,000 veteran entrepreneurs annually. Taking the helm as CEO in March of 2020 Hogan navigated the pandemic, social unrest, and economic instability to emerge as a stronger organization focused on solving one problem, creating access for entrepreneurs to resources, capital, and communities. Bunker solves this by building entrepreneurial communities and running programs based on the stage of participants businesses.

Prior to becoming the CFO, he co-founded and led Bunker Labs' Nashville and Austin chapters, where he helped foster a vibrant and supportive ecosystem for veteran innovation and economic opportunity. Additionally, Blake co-founded and successfully exited BreakAway Safety Solutions, a company that saves lives at outdoor events through portable emergency exits, protecting fans from potential disasters. The company was established as a response to the mass shooting during the Jason Aldean concert in Las Vegas. The exits safely have evacuated over 100,000 fans due to weather emergencies and at major events across the US.

Blake serves as a board member of the National Association of Veteran Owned Businesses. Finally, Hogan is a graduate of the Stand To Veterans Leadership Program at the George W. Bush Presidential Center. In this program, he gained insights from globally renowned leaders and experts, further fueling his commitment to effective leadership and service.

**BRENDAN ARONSON** graduated with distinction from The US Naval Academy and served as a Marine Infantry Officer for 6 years. He completed deployments to Japan and to Iraq as an advisor to the Iraqi Army during their fight against ISIS.

After the Marines, Brendan worked as an investment banker at Goldman Sachs, earned an MBA from The Wharton School in Philadelphia and launched 2 startups.

Brendan is a co-founder and CEO of The Military Veteran and a Venture Capital investor at Context Ventures, where he invests in military veteran founders. He lives in Los Angeles, California, and is an advocate for veterans in business.

**BRETT WHITSITT** grew up in the DC area through adolescence, Brett later went on to study Shakespeare and Victorian literature at the University of Oxford, and he was a Division-1 athlete (lacrosse) at the Virginia Military Institute, graduating with a degree in Economics & Business before joining the Navy. After service, Brett earned a Wharton MBA while working at J.P. Morgan (Leveraged Finance) before he became an entrepreneur and started multiple businesses.

As founder and CEO of a communications-oriented tech company for military and emergency response operations (Marvel fans out there, think *Jarvis...*), Brett brings a lot of experience to his role, built on a foundation of servant leadership and passion for national security. Drawing from his career as a SEAL Officer, having led troops in combat during 4 deployments and then directing special operations activity across 12 countries in Europe, he understands the life-threatening capability gaps associated with poor information flow during missions. Dedicated to preventing such challenges in the future, Squire Solutions incorporated in 2018.

Brett continues in his relentless endeavor to deliver better tools to our front lines, ultimately saving lives. He is also the co-owner & President of a veteran-led construction management firm. Any slice of free time is usually spent with his fiancé and their dog, *Stretch*!

**CARRIE ROEGER** has had a remarkable career, marked by her focus and determination to achieve success. Her journey began with five years of active duty in the US Marine Corps, where she made history as the first female Marine to be awarded the Navy/Marine Corps Gold Jump wings in 1993. After her military service, Carrie transitioned into the residential construction industry, starting as an administrative assistant and working her way up to become the Chief Operations Officer for a prominent residential developer. Throughout her tenure, Carrie excelled in areas such as strategic planning, operations, budget management, problem-solving, and training, earning recognition as an industry leader.

In 2015, Carrie and her Marine Corps-veteran husband co-founded the Semper Fi Bar and Grille, a restaurant that honors veterans, military personnel, first responders, and the community as a whole. This venture required Carrie to learn new skills in marketing, financial management, and leadership, leading to the restaurant's success in a challenging industry. Their accomplishments led the company to expand through the franchise business model in 2022. Carrie's dedication to business and community is also evident in her role as Chairman of the National Association of Home Builders 55+ Housing Council, where she provides leadership in addressing the housing needs of the aging population.

Continuing her pursuit of knowledge and growth, Carrie earned an MBA from the Jack Welch Management Institute at Strayer University in 2020. She also became an Adjunct Professor at Kennesaw State University, sharing her expertise in construction and architecture. In the same year, she founded White Stone Residential, LLC, a company focused on building quality homes in north Georgia. Currently, Carrie serves as a business coach and consultant at Shinn Consulting, a leading organization in the home building industry. Additionally, through her involvement in various organizations such as Vet To CEO and the Cherokee County Homeless Vets Program, Carrie leverages her resources and firsthand knowledge to support transitioning military personnel and veterans.

Carrie Roeger's journey has been marked by her unwavering dedication and continuous pursuit of success. From her groundbreaking achievements in the military to her prominent roles in the residential construction industry and community organizations, Carrie exemplifies focus, determination, and leadership. Her contributions as a business leader, coach, and advocate for veterans are testaments to her passion for helping others and making a meaningful impact.

**CHRISTOPHER ROHE** is the President/Co-Founder of Rogue Industries® and CEO/Co-Founder of GuardianSat™. Mr. Rohe provides an in-depth understanding of commercializing technologies for the business and government arena for multi-billion efforts with specific experience and expertise as a catalyst, thought leader, and innovator for new, novel, and transformative methods to seamlessly accelerate solutions focusing on: NextGen IT, Communications, Sensors, AI, Advanced Manufacturing & Construction, and Novel Testing/Training solutions with both government, DoD, and private industry accolades. As a business leader and certified general contractor Mr. Rohe has completed over 100 large-scale government projects and development effort of impact since 2000.

Mr. Rohe's academic excellence is demonstrated in his honors as a top graduate of the United States Air Force Academy, A master's degree in public policy from Harvard University's Kennedy School of government as well as earning Graduate Certificates in Business and Government Relations from Georgetown University's The Fund for American Studies and in AI, IP, and Computational Thinking from UPenn Engineering.

Mr. Rohe retired with over 20 years of service as an active duty and reserve officer in the USAF culminating with a Meritorious Service Medal for his leadership in the Test and Training Enterprise for advanced aircraft, communications, sensors, seekers, and platforms. He has achieved DoD certifications in numerous advanced programs and held all the requisite levels of sensitive clearances. As a program executive and acquisition officer overseeing multi-million and multi-billion-dollar next generation system programs, Mr. Rohe focused on the development of transformative technologies, large scale adaptive construction management programs, and specialized rapid government contracting solutions.

Prior to his current leadership of ROGUE® and GSAT™ Mr. Rohe was the Senior Business Development Manager for Advanced Programs at Lockheed Martin Missiles and Fire Control, Co-Founder and Senior Vice President of Strategy for Stryke Industries (a novel materials and manufacturing company) and served as a strategic consultant for several industry disruptors – and is a highly sought after (and published) national speaker on government innovation.

In his role with ROGUE® he has recently led over 40 large scale projects for the DoD culminating in – a $500M 5-year IDIQ Multiple Award Contract, $1B 5-year IDIQ Testing and Training Contract, $5B 5-year IDIQ Emerging Technologies Contract, and down-selection as a major technology company Mentor Protégé company. And in his role with GSAT™ he recently led the capture of a prestigious National Science Foundational (NSF) Small Business Innovation Award along with the Aerospace Corporation – a federally funded research and development center (FFRDC) for Space Innovations.

In addition to his business interest, Mr. Rohe was elected (and served a two year term) President of the Board of Directors for the 300-company National Advanced Mobility Consortium, sponsored by the Vehicle Robotics Alliance – Managed by the National Center for Manufacturing Sciences, and is the alumni President for his alma-maters w/n Florida and currently serves on Harvard Kennedy Schools Dean's Council, Reunion Team & Mentoring Programs and is a panel member for Senator Rick Scott's United States Air Force Academy's selection committee.

**CLINT MUSGROVE** was fascinated by the Army from a young age, even though military service was uncommon in his family. Like many Americans, the call to serve was solidified in the aftermath of the 9/11 terrorist attacks. Clint enlisted in the Army at the age of eighteen as a combat medic, serving two tours in Iraq before retiring in 2013. During his time in service, Clint was obsessively dedicated to the health and well-being of his fellow soldiers, known for his calm demeanor and sense of humor regardless of the circumstances.

After an overseas injury brought Clint's military career to a close, he pursued higher education while meticulously searching for new purpose. This path took unexpected turns as he found himself traversing multiple industries before arriving at the Department of Homeland Security, where he discovered that his experience and knowledge were well-suited for disaster management. Clint was able to add value within weeks of onboarding at FEMA as Hurricanes Harvey, Irma, and Maria devastated parts of the U.S. and its territories. After several years of federal service, Clint transitioned to the private sector, where he continues to provide solutions and reduce the complexity of incident response for a Fortune 500 energy provider.

Beyond his professional endeavors Clint is most passionate about his family, faith, and community. Additionally, he's a bit of a stoicism enthusiast. He hopes to inspire others to assign value to all that occurs throughout their journey, finding affirmation, especially in failure. He believes that, among all the ambitious goals one can set and achieve, the genuine measure of success lies in a person who prioritizes and cherishes his family above all else.

**DALLAS JAMISON**, USN, Ret. currently flies for FedEx Express as a First Officer on the MD-11. His love of aviation started at a young age and was solidified after his first flight at the age of eight. Since then, he has amassed over 5,000 flight hours and over 700 carrier arrested landings.

Dallas' military career started with his graduation from the United States Naval Academy in 2001 where he earned a Bachelor of Science in Quantitative Economics. After graduation, he attended flight school and was designated a Naval Aviator in 2004. Dallas went on to serve in various F/A-18 squadrons stationed both in the United States and overseas, conducting multiple combat deployments around the globe. He also served as an instructor at the Navy Fighter Weapons School (TOPGUN) and at the Pentagon on the Joint Staff as a strategic planner. Dallas retired from military service after having the privilege of serving as the Commanding Officer of Strike Fighter Squadron EIGHT ONE.

While aviation is a huge part of his life, Dallas' greatest love is his amazing wife, Suzanne, and their two children ages three and five. His hobbies include getting sleep when he can, working out, and watching college football. Dallas also really enjoys spending quality time with his family and being actively involved at his church.

**DAN JARVIS** first entered the U.S. Army at the age of 17 upon graduation from High School. He served 2 years, and then went to college graduating with a Bachelor's Degree in Criminology. Upon Graduation from college Dan became a Deputy Sheriff in Polk County, FL. When 9/11/2001 changed our world he opted to reenlist in the U.S. Army. Dan served as a combat infantryman deploying to Iraq and Afghanistan. Between the deployments he served as a Drill Sergeant at Ft. Knox, KY.

Dan was injured in combat in Afghanistan when he stepped on a pressure plate that detonated an Improvised Explosive Device only five feet from his position. Dan was awarded a Purple Heart for his traumatic brain injury. During his deployment to Afghanistan 4 of his men were medivaced four combat injuries not to return to the fight. One of the men from Dan's platoon was killed by a roadside bomb, Dan felt responsible for his death.

Dan was medically retired on September 11, 2014 for injuries sustained in combat. Dan returned to Law Enforcement for two additional years and had to retire due to combat injuries. In April 2018, Dan founded an organization called 22Zero, with the purpose of standing in the gap to provide healing for PTSD with veterans, first responders and their families. While at 22Zero they developed two very successful non-clinical interventions that heal the root injuries of PTSD, Anxiety and Depression. Treatment is no cost to mission clients and their immediate families. To date more than 10,000 men, women and children have found healing. Dan is the co-founder of Anxiety Guys, where they have brought their interventions to the civilian population. Anxiety Guys also trains, peer support for first responder agencies, pastoral counselors and licensed professionals.

Diana Villa. Her life journey began in Houston, TX, where she was born to Colombian parents. At the age of four, her family returned to their homeland, providing Diana with a culturally rich upbringing that lasted until she turned 15. Demonstrating remarkable determination, Diana graduated at the age of 17 and promptly enlisted in the United States Army as a combat medic, embarking on this transformative journey alongside her high school sweetheart.

Completing her four-year military commitment, Diana seamlessly transitioned to higher education. While supporting her husband's active-duty career, she earned a B.A. in Elementary Education, showcasing her resilience and dedication to both family and personal growth. Over the next two decades, Diana served as a military spouse and later took on the role of her husband's caregiver, embodying strength and commitment in every aspect of her life.

With a marital journey spanning 26 years, Diana and Andres are proud parents to three remarkable boys, aged 19, 16, and 7.

Diana's pursuit of knowledge continued beyond her undergraduate studies, culminating in a Master's in Organizational Leadership from Regent University. Her commitment to personal development is further exemplified by her credentials, including a life coaching certificate from the University of California and recognition as a Gallup Certified Strengths Coach.

Currently, Diana passionately serves her country as a peer leader and mentor for family support members with the Wounded Warrior Project. In addition to her dedication to military families, Diana is the proud owner of Thrive as Designed Coaching and Consulting Services, where she brings her expertise to empower individuals and organizations on their path to success.

**D.J. EAGLE BEAR VANAS** is a thought leader, celebrated speaker and best-selling author whose expertise is showing people and organizations how to apply the warrior spirit at work. He is the author of the best-selling book *The Tiny Warrior* which is printed in six countries and the novel *Spirit on the Run*. D.J.'s newest book, *The Warrior Within* was published by Penguin Random House in 2022.

D.J. is an enrolled member of the Ottawa Tribe and a former U.S. Air Force officer. He inspires organizations to strengthen their tribe and *practically apply* traditional warrior principles to serve at their best, stay resilient and lead with courage. For over two decades, he's delivered his dynamic programs to clients such as Walt Disney, NASA, Intel Corporation, the U.S. military, Amazon, Allstate, Costco, Mayo Clinic and over 500 tribal nations. He's also been invited to speak at The White House - twice.

He holds a B.S. from the U.S. Air Force Academy and an M.S. from University of Southern California and has served on the Board of Directors on the National Board of Certified Counselors. D.J. is featured on the PBS documentary *The Warrior Tradition*, exploring the warrior traditions across Indian Country, and was also the host of his own PBS special *Discovering Your Warrior Spirit*. D.J. has been featured in high-profile media outlets such as NBC, the Daily Stoic podcast, United Airlines *Hemispheres Magazine* and Forbes. He is also a regular contributing writer for *Men's Journal Magazine*.

**GARTH MASSEY** was commissioned in the Marine Corps through the Platoon Leaders Course program in 1996. Attended The Basic School, earning the MOS designation: 0302, Infantry Officer. He has served on Active duty and in the Reserves

As an infantry officer Garth has lead organizations from the platoon of 45 Marines to an infantry regiment of nearly 5,000 Marines and sailors. As a staff officer he has worked as the operations officer for a division planning the deployments, exercises and training for nearly 17,000. In these roles Col Garth has deployed around the world to include Asia, South America, The Middle East, and Africa with a combination of combat tours and humanitarian work.

Garth has a Bachelors in Speech communication, a master's in business administration (MBA) from Regis University in Denver Co and a Masters in Strategic Studies (MSS) from the Army War College in Charlie PA, he is a certified Operations and tactics instructor and holds numerous certifications in negotiations, planning and decision making.

Military awards include the Meritorious Service Medal (fourth award), Navy Commendation Medal (third award), Navy Achievement Medal (combat V and star) the Combat Action Ribbon as well as other personal, campaign and service awards.

Col Garth is the founder of CommandReady a learning and development firm teaching leadership nationally across industries like Construction, video gaming, law enforcement, healthcare and space. Additionally, He is the founder and CEO of a nonprofit 501(c)3 promoting veteran education and employment. In those roles he provides numerous keynote presentations on leadership and veteran issues. Serving on the board of directors for The Devil Pups and as a board of counselor for The University of Southern California's MBV graduate program. He is married to Kathleen Massey he lives in South Carolina with their six children.

**GENE MORAN,** founder and President of Capitol Integration, is the foremost expert on federal defense and security lobbying. He guides defense companies to dramatically improve federal sales through funding and policy change in Washington DC, measuring his client results in billions of dollars. Gene's policy initiatives have been implemented by Congress, The President and Executive branch agencies.

Gene's relentless pursuit of innovation has garnered multiple accolades. Capitol Integration is regularly recognized by Bloomberg Government as a Top-Performing Lobbying Firm and is twice-heralded by Florida State University as one of the 100 fastest growing alumni-led Florida companies. He is also twice recognized as a "Top Lobbyist" by the National Institute for Lobbying & Ethics, and a Top Ten Lobbyist by Gov Review. Gene is an inductee in the Million Dollar Consulting Hall of Fame ® and a recipient of the Society for Advancing Consulting's Consultant of the Year award.

Gene's groundbreaking research, exploring the impact of congressional lobbying on contracting and the performance of democracy, underpins a PhD in Public Policy and Administration. He is an adjunct Professor of Public Policy at Florida State University. Serving his country for 24 years in the Navy and in Washington DC, coupled with his strategic advisement and counsel to corporate leaders inspired Gene's podcast, Make Your Move, in support of veterans moving into industry, as well as Capitol Currency®, a unique learning program for corporate executives. A published author, Gene's latest book *Government Deals Are Funded, Not Sold: How to Integrate Lobbying in to Your Federal Sales Strategy* will be available from Taylor & Francis in November 2023.

**GEORGE KOVATCH** has earned a reputation over his 30-year federal career for helping organizations achieve results. George founded a Strategic Consulting and Congressional Relations company, KSA Federal, that specializes in helping companies and federal agencies navigate the federal budget and appropriations processes. He uses his Executive and Legislative branch relationships and experience to developing strategic plans and build teams that utilize business process improvement, evaluate data and risk, to inform investment decisions, drive organizational change, and achieve results.

George most recently served as the **Deputy Comptroller (Budget & Appropriations Affairs)/Deputy Under Secretary of Defense**, where he led a team of senior military officers and civilians responsible for delivering and securing congressional support for DoD's $700+ billion annual budget and advancing the Secretary of Defense's readiness and lethality priorities. His success earned him the Distinguished Public Service Award, the highest award the Secretary of Defense can give, noting "the numerous Department of Defense funding wins can be directly attributed to Mr. Kovatch's leadership and well-orchestrated collaboration."

Other Senior Executive Service positions include:

**Deputy Chief Management Officer/Deputy Under Secretary of the Navy (Management)**. During his tenure the Department of the Navy achieved $10 billion in savings over the Future Years Defense Program (FYDP), readiness for tactical aircraft increased from 50% to 80%, and the Department completed two full-scope CFO audits.

**Assistant Director, Federal Law Enforcement Training Centers (FLETC), Department of Homeland Security**. There he led their Washington, DC operations as the agency's representative before 100 federal partners, state, local, tribal, international, and private sector customers. He headed both FLETC's International Training division and Congressional relations team where he was responsible for achieving passage of FLETC's first Congressional Authorization Law in their 45-year history.

George worked in the private sector for a Management and IT consulting company where he led the business development efforts to successfully bring the company into two new markets: the Department of Homeland Security (DHS) and the Treasury Department.

George served on Capitol Hill on the **Senate Appropriations Committee, Subcommittee on Homeland Security**. The Subcommittee has jurisdiction over DHS' 22 agencies and appropriated over $45 billion annually.

He served on active duty in the U.S. Coast Guard for over 20 years as a surface operations specialist (Cutterman) in several ships in positions up through Commanding Officer. He was also a financial manager selected by the Commandant to establish a new office (CG-85) responsible for implementing the Service's financial management strategic plan. This set the stage for the Coast Guard and DHS to achieve an unqualified audit opinion for the first time in history.

A native of Massachusetts, George is a graduate of Boston College's Carroll School of Management and Columbia Business School's Executive MBA program.

**HEATHER THRONE** was born in Glen Ridge, NJ in 1972 and is the daughter of Alan and Nancy Marsh. Heather spent her early childhood growing up in New Jersey until her parents moved to Florida. Heather graduated from Jupiter High School in 1990 and went to the United States Military Academy at West Point, New York where in May 1994 she graduated with a B.S. degree in Environmental Sciences & Geography. During her time at West Point, Heather played on the women's soccer team for two years.

After graduation, she went to Fort Rucker (now Fort Novosel), Alabama to attend Initial Entry Rotary Wing (IERW) at the Army Aviation flight school. Following that phase, Heather was offered the opportunity to learn to fly the AH-64A Apache helicopters. She took on that challenge, completed the training and in 1995, moved to her first duty assignment at Fort Bragg (now Fort Liberty) with the 1/229th Attack Helicopter Battalion. While at the 1/229th, Heather had the opportunity to deploy to Bosnia in support of Operation Joint Guard. It was during her time at Fort Bragg that she met her husband, Tom, and they were married in 1998.

Following her assignment at Fort Bragg, Heather moved to South Korea where she served with the 6th Cavalry Regiment and then commanded the D, 3/6th Troop, consisting of over 100 soldiers. After her tour in South Korea and a final assignment in Alabama, Heather and her husband Tom decided to leave the military. Just before departing the U.S. Army, Heather earned a master's degree in human resources management from Troy University, Dothan, Alabama.

Heather worked for several different companies in various roles and levels of responsibility, including, Operations Management and Head of Human

Resources for a manufacturing company, most notably, Siemens. Heather continues to work for Siemens Healthineers, where she has work for over 14 years. Over the past 20 years, while working in corporate America, Heather managed the balancing act of work and raising four children, while her husband Tom continued to work for the federal government in an aviation role.

Today, Heather and Tom reside in Woodstock, Georgia where they are near empty nesters with only one of their four kids still at home. Their three sons are in college, Carson and Charlie are at the United States Coast Guard Academy and Ryan is studying architecture at Kennesaw State University. Their only daughter, Taylor is in middle school.

Heather continues to balance work and life, staying actively involved in her children's activities. She served as the president of the high school wrestling team parents' club for six years. Heather is also active today as a Girl Scouts co-leader, coaches at her local CrossFit gym, and enjoys hiking and traveling.

**J. SCOT HEATHMAN'S** life is marked by a desire to shoot for the skies. Raised in Minnesota with traditional Midwest values, he was an active participant in school, sports, and his community. However, his greatest passion emerged at just 3 years old, when he saw *Star Wars* in the theater for the first time. That day, he knew he was destined to fly airplanes. This dream prompted a 25-year career in the Air Force, during which time he became a highly decorated, combat instructor pilot and culminated as the installation commander of Scott Air Force Base and the Vice Commander of 18th Air Force, serving roughly 36,000 personnel.

Throughout his career, Scot learned the importance of relatability and resiliency, and became a respected servant leader. In 2019, however, that resiliency would be tested beyond anything he had ever experienced when he was involved in a car accident. After an MRI of his head and neck following the injuries he sustained, doctors discovered he had a brain tumor. The entire next year was spent in observation and assessment for further tumor growth and negative effects. In February 2020, his health took a turn for the worse, so he elected to go through a procedure to remove the tumor. After an eleven-hour surgery, most of the tumor was removed. Following 4-months of extensive therapy and healing, he returned to work, but had to undergo thirty rounds of radiation later that Fall, while still serving as the Base Commander. This experience taught him how impactful his own lessons could be in inspiring others and prompted a unique opportunity to elevate others who faced adversity. So, in 2022, he retired from the Air Force and set out to bring his own ideas of courage and a proven leadership style to help leaders better command themselves and their own cultures and organizations.

Today, Scot inspires CEO's to front-line leaders to 'command with courage' so they can lead more effectively, drive a culture of innovation, and build a bigger bottom line. His Commander level coaching programs inspire his clients to lead with relatability and respect to embrace their vulnerability for positive change. Scot possesses master's degrees in organizational leadership, Operational Planning & Strategy, and National Security & Strategic Studies, and is certified in emotional intelligence and executive coaching, designed to take leadership performance to the highest altitudes. His tireless efforts and performance earned him recognition by the International Association of Top Professionals as the 2024 Top Emotional Intelligence Consultant and Retired Colonel of the Year award. He's also the author of the upcoming book "Command With Courage" about resilience and elevating beyond adversity.

**JAMES "BART" BARTELLONI** is a proud graduate of the US Naval Academy, where he earned a Bachelor of Science in Mathematics. His post-academy career he was a Naval Aviator flying F-14 A/B/D Tomcats, serving in four consecutive squadrons without ever leaving the cockpit. A distinguished Naval Aviator, he is a graduate of the US Navy Fighter Weapons School (TOPGUN) and has deployed multiple times to global hotspots, primarily focusing on Iraq and the Arabian Gulf. His exemplary service has been recognized through numerous leadership awards in every squadron, along with multiple Air Medals and other commendations.

After his tenure in the Navy, Bartelloni transitioned to entrepreneurship, where his pursuit of radical innovation has led to the successful establishment and sale of various companies, alongside valuable learning experiences from his ventures. His current focus is revolutionizing the clinical development market through a comprehensive healthcare platform designed to streamline all phases of clinical trials along with exploring the impact of AI. Beyond his business endeavors, Bartelloni is deeply committed to supporting veterans and active-duty service members. He co-founded the non-profit SUP Vets, (www.thesupvets.org) where he merges his leadership skills with his passion for Stand-Up Paddle Surfing. This initiative aims to recreate the camaraderie experienced in the military, allowing veterans to connect with the therapeutic power of the ocean and forge lasting friendships. Furthermore, his involvement with the Bonefrog Foundation (www.bff4vets.com ), where he serves on the Board of Advisors, is a testament to his dedication to introducing holistic healing practices and alternative therapies to veterans, offering them options beyond conventional medicine.

Bartelloni's personal life is as fulfilling as his professional one. He cherishes his marriage to his high school sweetheart, and together they are the proud parents of four incredible children and the grandparents of five wonderful grandchildren.

**JOE MUSSELMAN** is an American venture capitalist, entrepreneur, and non-profiteer. He focuses on building, advising, and investing in extraordinary Teams, Leadership, and Culture (TLC). Joe's investment and director experience is extensive and diverse, including board roles at the NASDAQ, national non-profits and endowment funds, and companies ranging from early-formation stages to multi-billion market cap companies across several industries and sectors. He has served as special advisor to two sitting U.S. Presidents and the U.S. Senate and Congress members. As a result of his life's work, Joe has been recognized by multiple global publications such as Bloomberg, TechCrunch, WSJ, NYT, Forbes, CNN Tech, and Business Insider for his work in partnership and talent strategies, leadership, and corporate culture. Joe graduated from DePaul University (Chicago, IL). Joe is a classical violinist and a Merit School of Music graduate. He graduated from Fenwick H.S. and DePaul University. Later in life, he received Executive Certificates from Harvard, Stanford, Yale, and Pepperdine. Joe has lectured at NYU, UCSD, and UCLA, on his favorite topic: The Art and Science of Teams, Leadership, and Culture. Joe lives in Chicago with his wife and two beautiful and strong-willed children, Jack (4) and Sofia (2), with one on the way in July 2024.

**JOHN KEATING** has called Frisco home since 1999 and have had the honor of serving on your Frisco City Council since 2010. Once elected, I went to work on several of our city's most important projects, including the Dallas Cowboys partnership at The Star, opening the National Soccer Hall of Fame with FC Dallas, renewing the NCAA Division 1 Football Championship contract with Frisco, opening the University of North Texas Frisco campus, renewing the NCAA Division 1 Football Championship contract with Frisco, opening our new state-of-the-art library, and bringing the PGA Headquarters to Frisco.

I served in the US Army for 13 years as a senior counterintelligence agent, where I received the best leadership training in the world. In 1990, I was deployed to Saudi Arabia as part of "Operations Desert Shield and Desert Storm." For my military and community service, I was awarded a "Congressional Veteran Commendation" by Congressman Sam Johnson in 2017 and was recognized by Pepsi Frito-Lay with the "Valor Leadership Award" in 2016 for my work with various Veteran organizations. I continue to serve my country by serving my community.

In 2010 I was recognized by the Frisco ISD PTA with the "Texas Congress of Parents and Teachers Honorary Lifetime Membership Award" for my PTA fundraising work on behalf of local teachers and students from 2003 to 2010. I am the proud father of two sons - Zach and Ryan.

**JULIANA MERCER** is a Marine Corps veteran who served her country honorably in and out of war zones for sixteen years. Throughout her military career, she deployed to Iraq and Afghanistan and spent four years providing holistic support to injured Marines recovering at the Wounded Warrior Battalion in San Diego. After active duty, she channeled her passion and experience into the Veteran nonprofit arena, where she has actively supported wounded warriors and veterans' reintegration into civilian life. With over 20 years of experience working with and serving the veteran population, Juliana is deeply committed to serving their unique interests and needs. She knows what it takes to help veterans thrive.

In her quest to help fellow veterans and herself heal from years of personal and military trauma, Juliana found relief through psychedelic therapy that fundamentally changed her life. Having experienced its healing potential firsthand, she now dedicates her time and energy to ensuring that veterans who suffer from complex, chronic PTSD also have access to these therapies. Thus, in her current role as Director of Veteran Advocacy & Public Policy for the nonprofit organization Healing Breakthrough, Juliana passionately advocates for the research, training, and deployment of system-wide adoption of MDMA-Assisted Therapy in the U.S. Department of Veterans Affairs.

In addition, Juliana serves on the Heroic Hearts Project board of directors and is a lifetime member of the VFW, American Legion, and Marine Memorial Club.

**JULIE VIDA** is a technology thought leader and business executive specializing in the government and public sector space. Her most recent role was Group Vice President & Chief Strategy Advisor - Public Sector at Splunk (NYSE: SPLK). She and her team of advisors provided guidance and thought leadership with customers, partners and the public around the business and mission value outcomes delivered by the Splunk Data platform. Prior to joining Splunk, Julie was a Vice President at IT research giant Gartner in the Executive Programs practice, advising and coaching federal government Chief Information Officers (CIO) and IT senior leaders.

Before her career pivot to technology in the private sector, she served honorably for 24 years in the US Navy, retiring as a Commander in 2012. Initially a top student in Russian at the Defense Language Institute, she switched tracks to the Officer community and entered the US Naval Academy. Earning her commission in 1994, she then served 20 years as both a Surface Warfare Officer and Naval Aviator (helicopter pilot), serving in various combat ships and helicopter squadrons. Her highest military award is the Navy Air Medal, recognizing her superior airmanship and bravery in armed conflict, earned during Operation ENDURING FREEDOM in the earliest days following the 9/11 terrorist attacks. Her final role in government was as the Navy's Deputy Chief Information Officer in the Pentagon where she led policy and governance over technology investments and implementation and cybersecurity.

Julie has served on several advisory boards in both the defense and higher education sectors. Notably, as the fourth woman in USNA history to be elected as a Trustee on the US Naval Academy Alumni Association's Board of Trustees, she represented the highest concentration of living

Naval Academy alumni in the Maryland/Virginia/Washington DC region. She gives freely of her time mentoring and guiding transitioning military veterans of all ranks as they leave the service for private industry, helping them identify their skills, talents and desires to pursue their best lives after the military. Passionate about supporting and encouraging women and girls in technology, she also volunteers and speaks at events to encourage pursuit of STEM career fields, building confidence, and learning through setbacks.

A lover of word puzzles and trivia games, she is a former champion of two televised game shows, "The Weakest Link" and "Wheel of Fortune."

**KATHERINE ROWE** is busy applying the leadership and problem-solving skills she honed as an officer in the U.S. Army, Katherine has led projects for a diverse portfolio of clients in major U.S. sports leagues and college athletics, helping them to become more data-driven to engage fans and grow the bottom line.

In addition to her time in the military, Katherine brings a unique perspective to the sports industry as a former NCAA Division III student athlete and field hockey captain at Clark University in Worcester, Massachusetts.

Katherine is passionate about sports and her past professional experiences include working as an analyst and strategic consultant to sports organizations including the San Antonio Spurs, ESPN, the NBA Summer League, Hall Pass Media, and the University of Texas Longhorns and careers at Kraft Analytics Group and Salesforce.

**KIRSTEN BRUNSON** served on active duty in the US Army for almost 24 years. She earned a B.A. in Criminology from the University of Maryland and a J.D. from UCLA, where she was on the Law Review. She holds a LL.M. with a specialty in Military Justice from the Judge Advocate General's (JAG) Legal Center and School. Her assignments in the JAG Corps include serving as Deputy Chief of the Defense Appellate Division and Deputy Staff Judge Advocate for US Army Special Operations Command. In 2008, Colonel Brunson was selected as the first African American female to serve as an Army judge. She served as a Circuit Judge at Fort Hood, TX and Fort Bragg, NC presiding over courts-martial in Texas, Louisiana, Oklahoma, North Carolina, South Carolina, and Georgia. Her awards and decorations include the Parachutist's Badge, Legion of Merit, Meritorious Service Medal, Shield of Sparta (National Infantry Association), and Keeper of the Hourglass (7th Infantry Division). She was inducted into the Army Women's Foundation Hall of Fame in 2021.

Kirsten has remained active in the community since retirement. She is a member of The Links, Inc. (Tacoma, WA chapter). She volunteers as an advisor to the Spouses' Club of Lewis McChord, Honorary Chairperson of both the Fort Lewis Thrift Shop and Scholarship Board, and Merit Badge Counselor and Advancement Chair for the Pacific Harbors Council Troop

62, Boy Scouts of America. She also chairs the Military and Veterans Committee of the National Association of Women Judges. In 2022, she began serving on the Secretary of Defense's Military Justice Review Panel. Most recently, she was chosen to serve on the Design Advisory Council for the Global War on Terrorism Memorial Foundation. Kirsten has previously served as a homeschool teacher, private school board chair, and Director of Children's Ministry at her church.

Kirsten is married to Lieutenant General Xavier Brunson. The Brunson's have two adult daughters and a son in high school. Kirsten spends any free time with their Labradoodle.

**LARISA HARRINGTON**, PCC, C-IAYT, is a passionate and dedicated High-Performance and Well-Being Coach, Consultant, Trainer and Speaker, committed to helping purpose-driven professionals feel better, and perform better so they can make a bigger impact in the world without burning out. She is a Professional Certified Coach, Certified Yoga Therapist & 20-year Air Force retiree with over 2 decades of experience working in wellness & leadership and specializes in mindfulness, emotional intelligence, holistic stress management, somatic trauma healing, and conscious leadership.

Larisa began her military career in the intelligence field and then transitioned to an employee assistance role teaching leadership, well-being and resiliency to both military and civilians supporting the National Security Agency until retiring in 2017. She has a deep understanding of how high-stress environments affect the productivity, effectiveness, health and well-being of those who have dedicated their life to serving others. During her time in the military, she supported the well-being of thousands of military members, and continues to work for the Air Force Wounded Warrior Program coaching service members who have been wounded, ill or injured. Although no longer on active duty, Larisa is committed to being of service and positively contributing to the world.

Larisa is the owner/founder of Strong By Nature Wellness, a holistic well-being company offering 1:1 and group coaching, healing, yoga & strategy to help purpose-driven professionals improve their peace, presence and productivity. She is also the owner/founder of Better Execs, an executive coaching and consulting company providing 1:1 coaching, consulting and trainings to support purpose-driven organizations committed to the well-being & success of their people & their organization. Larisa lives in New Market, Maryland with her husband, Quinn, son, Donovan, daughter, Gabriella, and mother, Rochelle, along with their dog, gecko and snake. When she's not working, Larisa enjoys hiking places with stunning views, lifting heavy weights, traveling the world to find the best coffee gelato, watching sunrises and sunsets over the water, and volunteering with horses, dogs and cats.

**LAURA NOEL** is an Organizational Development consultant, ICF leadership coach, and a senior consultant and facilitator with The Arbinger Institute as well as an International Best-Selling Author and Podcast Host. Prior to launching her business, Stretch Into Success, Laura served in the United States Air Force for more than 27 years, rising to the rank of Chief Master Sergeant. She spent much of her Air Force career teaching personal growth and leadership.

Since retiring from the Air Force, Laura has served as a consultant to organizations, individuals, and solopreneurs to streamline business processes while maximizing effectiveness, alignment, and impact. She helps clients stretch their thinking and mindsets in a way that opens them up to new possibilities.

Laura is a PsyD candidate in the field of Leadership Psychology and Neuroscience at William James College, where she serves as adjunct faculty. She has continued to develop her expertise as a coach and consultant through her studies. She also worked closely with her mentor, the late Bob Proctor, for years. Proctor who was a world-renowned expert in human potential and success.

**MARK ZINNO** is national and local sports media host that has worked for some of the biggest names in the industry to include ESPN, CBS Sports Radio and Vegas Stats & Information Network. His work is multi-platform on television, radio and digital. Mark is also a 24-year Servicemember in the United States Army on active duty, the Reserves and National Guard. He has served multiple combat deployments and commanded at the highest levels of the organization.

Mark also gives back his time working in the veteran non-profit space weekly sitting down with veterans to increase their mental and physical healthy and help provide them with a variety of services to increase their quality of life.

While continue to still serve in uniform, Mark has combined his love of military service and his passion for broadcasting into highly successful podcast called the "Hazard Ground." This show tells tales of combat and survival from a first-person point of view and has expanded to discuss a variety of topics including PTSD, veterans suicide, currently military affairs and more. He has interviewed multiple Medal of Honor recipients, politicians, authors, movie stars, entrepreneurs and more! The Hazard Ground has featured someone from every major US military engagement since World War II and has a worldwide audience.

**MARLENE "MARLIE" ANDERSCH** is the CEO & Founder of rockITdata. An Air Force Veteran with over 30 years of technology experience. Marlie has a competitive spirit and a set of core values that have driven her from climbing the corporate ladder at other technology companies to become founder and CEO of rockITdata, a certified woman, minority, and veteran-owned business that provides data integrations, AI/ML services in the contact center leveraging Amazon Web Services and Salesforce development.

Established four years ago, Marlie hit the ground running with rockITdata and grew her company from 4-5 employees to over 175 employees and counting within the past year. Through persistence, taking leaps of faith, surrounding herself with key leaders and following her core values, Marlie has built a business that has roots in who she is. Those roots have allowed her company, partners, and those on her staff to understand their own core values while always pushing themselves to think differently.

**MATTHEW GRIFFIN** served four combat tours in Afghanistan and Iraq with the storied 2nd Ranger Battalion, departing the military in 2006 to create positive, sustainable change in conflict areas. With the skills learned in the military, Griff co-founded Combat Flip Flops; manufactured fashion and lifestyle products in war zones, used profits to fund girls education, cleared land mines, and supported veteran charities. The company that everybody thought would fail created a moving TEDx talk, successfully secured Mark Cuban as a partner on Shark tank, and funded education for over 1000 girls in Northern Afghanistan.

In addition to building a globally respected philanthropic brand, Griff was a member of the first team to successfully ski off the tallest mountain in Iraq in the award winning Film, Adventure Not War: Ski Iraq. In 2019, Griff lead and executive produced the film, Here Am I, Send Me, a Sundance recognized film that follows the trail of Griff and fellow Rangers freefalling a Gold Star Mother into the opening ceremonies of the 75th Anniversary of D-Day.

Griff is a husband, father of two daughters, and dog lover.

**MEAGHAN MOBBS**, PhD, is an experienced nongovernmental, policy and political leader. She's a graduate of West Point, holds a Master in forensic psychology from George Washington University and a doctorate in clinical psychology from Columbia University. A Tillman Scholar and George W. Bush Veteran Leadership Scholar, she previously served as a Presidential appointee to the United States Military Academy- West Point Board of Visitors and is a Gubernatorial appointee to the Virginia Military Institute Board of Visitors.

A senior fellow on American safety and security at Independent Women's Forum, she has advised numerous state and national decision-makers on defense, national security, and foreign policy issues. As a humanitarian, she's chartered relationships with the US Government, multi-national governments, legacy nongovernmental organizations, and donors to project American values around the world.

Meaghan is known for her research into understanding the unique psychosocial stressors of service during a time of war and has frequently published on this topic. Meaghan is a former paratrooper and combat veteran who serves on the Board of multiple organizations dedicated to assisting service members in the transition to civilian life.

**MICAH NIEBAUER** is originally from Superior, Wisconsin. He attended college at Wheaton College, IL, majored in Political Science, and was a member of the ROTC program. Upon graduation in 2003, he worked at both the U.S. Department of State and the U.S. Department of Commerce prior to beginning service in the U.S. Army as an Infantry Officer in the 82d Airborne Division. He later joined the Special Forces and served in the 3rd Special Forces Group (Airborne). Micah completed multiple tours in support of the Global War on Terror before resigning his commission in June of 2014 to pursue an entrepreneurial path and open Southern Pines Brewing Company.

He is currently the CEO of Southern Pines Brewing Company which has grown from a single site to four locations either open or in development. Micah completed a Master of Business Administration at The Wharton School, University of Pennsylvania in 2019, and is currently enrolled in the Owner/President Management Program at Harvard Business School. Micah serves on the board of the Moore County Economic Development Partnership, Penick Village Life Plan Community, and the North Carolina Craft Brewers Guild.

Micah and his wife Patricia have been married for 17 years and have three children, Eva (14), and Claudia (11), and Wyatt (8). Patricia is a partner at Robins, May, and Rich LLP in Pinehurst, and they reside in Southern Pines.

**MICHELLE CURRAN** led an impressive career as a Fighter Pilot during her 13 years in the United States Air Force. From 2019-2021, she flew as the only female pilot for the Air Force Thunderbirds and performed for millions across the country and internationally. Michelle has been featured on several well-known media platforms, including The Kelly Clarkson Show, CBS Evening News, and Glamour. But before stepping into the spotlight with the Thunderbirds, Michelle was a combat proven fighter pilot completing missions across Europe, Asia, and the Middle East.

As the Lead Solo for the Thunderbirds, Michelle realized the flying was cool, but the best part was inspiring others to overcome their fears and pursue their dreams. Since transitioning out of the military, she has founded her company, Upside Down Dreams, and is committed to empowering men and women of all ages to overcome obstacles and face their self-doubt head on. She has inspired thousands from the stage and become an in-demand international speaker.

Michelle's passion for breaking barriers and setting the example of what can be accomplished through hard work inspired her to write her first children's book, also named Upside Down Dreams. The first in a three-book series, this story has empowered kids to chase their dreams despite the fear that may stand in their way. Since then, Michelle has become a best-selling author and an in-demand international speaker known for her relatability and authenticity despite her impressive background.

**MIKE SARRAILLE** is a globally top-rated leadership and organizational culture subject matter expert, best-selling author, keynote speaker, entrepreneur, and extreme adventurer. He specializes in guiding small- and medium sized businesses to Fortune 500 companies on leadership, culture, and high-performing teams.

Mike earned his bachelor's degree in Business Administration from Texas A&M University in 2003 and his MBA from the McCombs School of Business at the University of Texas in 2017. He is the founder and CEO of Talent War Group, a Leadership Development & Executive Search firm, and co-founder of Legacy Expeditions. This extreme adventure firm recently set 4 x world records for skydiving all seven continents in 6 days, 6 Hours, and 6 minutes. He is also the co-author of the best-selling book, 'The Talent War: How Special Operations and Great Organizations Win on Talent,' and author of the recently released book, 'The Everyday Warrior: A No-Hack Practical Approach to Life.' Mike also leads the Men's Journal Everyday Warrior initiative to inspire greatness through a practical, no-frills approach to living a more fulfilling and purpose-driven life.

Mike's extensive military background includes being a retired U.S. Navy SEAL officer, former enlisted Recon Marine, and Scout-Sniper. He completed Basic Underwater Demolition/SEAL (BUD/S) Training. He served in SEAL Team THREE, leading historic combat operations during the Battle of Ramadi in 2006 and the Battle of

Sadr City in 2008. Mike served as the SEAL Junior Officer Training Course (JOTC) Director, where he mentored and prepared junior SEAL officers to lead combat operations. Mike was then assessed and selected for assignment to the Naval Special Warfare Development Group (DEVGRU) to support global counter terrorism operations. He completed ten combat deployments supporting the Global War on Terrorism. He was awarded the Silver Star, six Bronze Stars for Valor, two Defense Meritorious Service Medals, and a Purple Heart.

Global Gurus ranked Mike among the World's Top 30 Leadership Professionals in 2023. Mike shares stories and lessons learned from his time as a military and business leader that will take you on a thrilling journey through the highs and lows of building and leading high-performing, elite teams. Each of his accounts contains valuable lessons that will broaden your understanding of leadership development, talent acquisition, talent management, organizational culture, teamwork, overcoming adversity, accountability, and positively impacting those around you.

**MISTY COOK** serves as the Chief Executive Officer of Concierge on Call, affectionately known as The COC. In her leadership role at this consulting firm, Misty specializes in guiding retired General/Flag Officers and senior leaders through the intricate steps of transitioning from military service to establishing their own thriving consulting enterprises. She plays a crucial role in preparing these individuals to leave a lasting and distinguished impression, facilitating a seamless transition, and providing the tools and strategies to create opportunities for post-retirement income that align with their lifestyle goals.

Leveraging her extensive background in administrative support, adept meeting planning, and a robust network of business connections, Misty assists leaders in securing speaking engagements and opportunities for board memberships. Her team collaborates with senior leadership, presidents, and chief executive officers, delivering executive assistance services that support business growth and maintain their professional reputation with numerous prestigious corporations globally.

As a former Marine Officer, Misty's portfolio spans diverse projects, ranging from developing innovative processes for startups to meticulously planning and executing events for foreign dignitaries, state and federal representatives, and industry leaders across the United States and abroad.

Beyond her corporate responsibilities, Misty shares her insights as a speaker at consulting firms and armed forces events, earning recognition as an expert in military protocol, event planning, and dining etiquette. Currently residing in Washington, DC, Misty Cook brings a wealth of expertise and leadership to the heart of the nation's capital.

**MOLLY JENKS** was born in Vicenza, Italy and is the child of third generation Army officer's. She graduated from Xavier University in Cincinnati, OH with a degree in biochemistry. Upon graduation, Molly was commissioned into the United States Army as a Signal Corps 2nd Lieutenant. Molly served many worldwide locations to include South Korea, Germany, Australia, Hawaii, Iraq, Italy among others. Halfway through her military career, she took advantage of the opportunity to change from the Signal Corps to the Nuclear and Counterproliferation branch of the Army. She retired from the Army at 20 years. She has pursued a civilian career in consulting for the government.

The main projects Molly focused on in her military career were the Department of Defense transition to Everything Over Internet Protocol (EoIP), Operation Iraqi Freedom and the transference of power to local governance, UN Security Resolution 1540 Cooperative Training, and the Immediate Liquid Fast Culture Study. She has continued her work in Communications and counterproliferation in roles on the Joint Staff and at the Defense Threat Reduction Agency. She spends most of her personal time volunteering with the Childrens Hospital at the National Institutes of

Health, educating about the importance of organ donation of as a foster rottweiler dog volunteer family.

In March of 2020, Molly was diagnosed with an extremely rare, aggressive, terminal form of non-Hodgkin's lymphoma. She received a Stem Cell transplant and has now become the first survivor of her cancer. Molly will celebrate both her 50th birthday and 4 years cancer free this year.

**NEAL CONLON** was raised in New York City and thrived in its ethos of diversity. NYC was my first school of hard knocks. It created a deep interest in understanding humans from all walks of life.

As he grew into a young man, he felt lost and broken within.He believed enlisting in the US Marines was the medicine he needed at the time. The Marines instilled discipline, leadership principles, situational awareness, and provided him with brotherhood. Although it prepared him for life in many ways, he could still feel something missing.

After leaving the marines, his ego chased status and success in some of the world's most powerful companies including Guugenheim Partners, Cushman & Wakefield, Morgan Stanley, and NBC. He rose above the ranks and went on to achieve all my goals, except, doing so, did not feel right. Something was still missing.

Compelled to end his suffering, he committed to his healing by incorporating multi-disciplinary practices and tools to heal himself and find the answers he was seeking. He pressed *forward* past the adversity in my life to go onto live the life of my dreams. It is now his mission to awaken others to the knowledge and power within each one of us to live a meaningful life. Once we press forward we are able to align with our purpose and access the medicine within all of us

Patrick George is the President and Board Director of Hover Energy, a pioneering wind technology company focused on seamlessly integrating wind, solar, and battery storage into urban environments. Concurrently, he serves as the Managing Partner of Beachwood Ventures, a venture capital and advisory firm established in 2018. Patrick's expertise lies in fundraising, strategy, operations, and talent acquisition. In addition to his leadership roles, he serves on the LP Committee for Arcadian Capital, advises Mineral Answers, and mentors at Capital Factory in Austin, Texas. From 2015 to 2020, Patrick served as the Co-Founder and President of Accelerate Resources, a technology- and data-driven energy company specializing in upstream oil and gas asset acquisition. Backed by $300 million from Pine Brook Partners, Accelerate achieved a top 7% portfolio in the U.S. through 150 acquisitions. Despite navigating two significant oil price crashes, Patrick successfully negotiated an additional $100 million in capital investment.

Patrick's commitment to service extends to his distinguished career in the United States Marine Corps since 2005. Having completed two combat tours in Iraq and commanded a Recon Company, he is a two-time recipient of the Navy & Marine Corps Commendation Medal. Patrick, currently a Major in the Marine Innovation Unit, holds academic achievements from the Marine Corps University's Command & Staff College and Expeditionary Warfare School.

Patrick holds an MBA from Cornell University's SC Johnson College of Business, where he was a Roy H. Park Leadership Fellow and Nolan Scholar. He earned his BA in Economics and Government from the University of Texas at Austin, receiving the Frank J. Ruck Leadership Award. Patrick's accolades include the 10 Under 10 Notable Alumni by the Cornell Johnson School of Management, an EY Entrepreneur of the Year® nominee, a Dallas Business Journal 40 under 40 awardee, and an Oil and Gas Investor Forty under 40 honoree. Patrick is a member of the Young Presidents' Organization and the National Council for the American Enterprise Institute. In his free time, he enjoys fly fishing, racket sports, and geopolitics.

**ROBERT HAMILTON OWENS** was the Chaplain for Football, Baseball and Basketball at the University of Nevada-Reno for 22 years. He founded and Senior Pastored a Non Denominational church for 25 years , growing the church to 3000 attendees. At 32 yeas old, and was appointed by two Governors to the Nevada State Judicial Ethics Commission, and ran for the Nevada State Legislature. His efforts also included working with inmates in five Prisons in Nevada and California.

Robert has been a Leadership and Management Consultant for 35 years. Robert has Coached and Consulted in 30 nations. He once hosted a weeekly one hour Television Program on FOX Affiliate called "Leadership for Changing Times" for 22 years. Robert is presently is a Mental Resilience or Mental Toughness and Self Mastery Coach for Business Leaders, Military and Athletes across the Country and internationally.. He also trains USAF Pararescue and Special Operations Military candidates today for SEALFIT, and is a Professional Developmental trainer for The Pararescue Foundation. Robert is often referred to as "The Legend".

Robert has been mentioned often as possibly the greatest endurance athlete in the US in the last 100 years. He has been competing as an Endurance Athlete for now over 50 years. One of the Original Ironman Triathletes: He did year 3 of Ironman back in 1980 in Honolulu. His illustrious career includes 12 Ironmans and 6 half Ironmans. Robert also completed the Ironman World Championships in Kona in 2003.

At 66 Robert completed the "300 of Sparta" endurance event. They ran-walked 238 miles across Greece in 8 days. He also completed the World Marathon Challenge or 777: 7 Marathons in 7 Days on 7 Continents. Over his lifetime, he has competed in 20 marathons. At 71, Robert was the only American on a European Team that rowed across the Atlantic from

December 6th 2022 till January 16th 2023. His efforts raised awareness and funds for Veterans Suicide Prevention Awareness Programs. Robert completed SEALFIT's 50 Hour non stop Navy SEAL led Crucible Event called "Kokoro". Oldest athlete to ever attempt it or finish it.

Joe De Sena, the founder of Spartan Games, declared that "Robert Owens was the Fittest and Mentally Toughest 66 Year Old in the World." Triathlete Magazine referred to him as "The Most Interesting Triathlete in the World!"

## ROBERT "TYLER" VAN HOOK, a Virginia native, embodies grit and

resilience. Enlisting in the U.S. Marine Corps at 17, he distinguished himself through intense training and swift advancement. His career highlights include serving in Marine Reconnaissance and Marine Special Operations, with deployments in Iraq, Afghanistan, and the Arabian Peninsula. His leadership skills and tactical acumen in diverse combat zones underscore his exceptional military career.

Transitioning from military to academic excellence, Van Hook pursued a bachelor's in strategic studies and defense analysis at Norwich University. His academic journey continued as a Faculty Advisor at Marine Corps University, shaping future military minds. Presently, he's enriching his knowledge with a master's at Brown University, demonstrating his commitment to lifelong learning and personal growth.

Beyond his military and academic endeavors, Van Hook co-founded Kognitiv Edge, blending his military expertise with innovative business strategies. His personal life is as dynamic as his career, enjoying fitness activities and cherishing moments with his wife and their three dogs. Van Hook's journey from a young Marine to a multifaceted leader and entrepreneur encapsulates a story of determination, adaptability, and unwavering dedication.

## SAL FILARDI is originally from New Haven, CT and grew up near Chicago,

IL. The son of a nurse and an engineer, he was taught to value serving others and improving processes from a young age. He is a proud graduate of Marmion Academy where he played football and was a member of the Drill Team. He studied Communication at the University of Illinois and put theory immediately to practice at his college jobs as a manager of a bar and emergency maintenance person for campus apartments. With his diploma, he also earned a commission as a Field Artillery Officer in the US Army.

Sal served in the 1st Cavalry Division at Ft. Hood (Cavazos), TX with a mechanized infantry company as a Fire Support Officer. He led a Fire Direction Center for an artillery battery and was the Radar Platoon Leader for his brigade. His time in the artillery was highlighted by a 9-month rotation to South Korea where he embedded with a Korean artillery unit and participated in a large, multinational military demonstration near the DMZ.

Motivated by what he learned working closely with a foreign military, as well as his high-performing peers, he applied for the mentally and physically rigorous Special Forces Assessment and Selection. After gaining an invite to the Qualification Course, he earned his Green Beret in 2019. He served with 3rd Special Forces Group at Ft. Bragg (Liberty), NC, where he led his Detachment on multiple training and advisory missions in West Africa. He finished his time in uniform as an executive officer for the Technical Support Company and as a member of a joint staff while deployed to the Middle East.

Sal now spends his time as a management consultant at GreenCastle Consulting. He translates the tools he used in Special Operations to help business leaders create clarity and alignment by implementing operational best practices that drive results. He is honored to be married to Jess, a proud Texas Longhorn and Project Manager at Oracle's NetSuite. He volunteers with organizations that support entrepreneurs and youth athletes. He's most likely to be found in the suburbs of Philadelphia with his three small children, pulling a wagon toward to the nearest playground or putting green.

**SHANNON POTTS** is a native of Illinois and enlisted in the Marine Corps in April 2001 and attended Recruit Training in Parris Island, SC in January 2002 graduating Platoon Honor Graduate and earning meritorious promotion. During Shannon's early military service, she served as an avionics calibration and repair technician deploying to Okinawa, Japan for six months and later with the 13th MEU, serving part of that deployment aboard Al Asad Air Base, Iraq in support of Operation IRAQI FREEDOM.

Upon return, Shannon reported to the Naval Reserve Officer Training Corps at the University of Illinois at Urbana-Champaign as a student. Shannon commissioned as a Second Lieutenant in October of 2009. As an officer, Shannon served as an Adjutant and was assigned to Combat Logistics Regiment 2 aboard Camp Lejeune, NC; later serving with 2d Marine Logistics Group.

In late 2013, Shannon transitioned from active duty to the reserve component. During this time, Shannon served her growing family while supporting her husband's job transition, which brought them to San Antonio, Texas. In early 2017, Shannon joined 1st Battalion, 23d Marine Regiment out of Houston, Texas, later applying to return to full-time service in the Active Reserve program. This brings her to where she currently serves as the Manpower Officer with 23d Marine Regiment in San Bruno, CA.

Shannon's personal decorations include the Navy and Marine Corps Commendation Medal (second award), Navy and Marine Corps Achievement Medal, the Military Outstanding Volunteer Service Medal and various other Service and Campaign medals.

Shannon is married to John G. Potts, and they have six children; two of which are also currently serving in the Armed Forces. Shannon possesses a true passion for helping others and enjoys running, CrossFit, and spending time with the family outdoors.

**STACY RASKE** is a bestselling author, speaker, podcast host, Iraq War Veteran, peak performance coach, energy optimization expert, executive coach, leadership mentor, and business & systems strategist. She helps impact-driven leaders and organizations optimize and systematize to elevate their performance, people, and profit. She empowers Alpha Leaders and Driven Disruptors to embrace their inner rebel and leverage their genius to shatter the status quo.

Her mission in life is to unlock the highest potential and performance in others by shattering the invisible ceiling so they can embody their full purpose while enjoying the ride. Stacy has written for and been featured in numerous magazines, including Authority Magazine, Yahoo Finance, and Business Insider.

Using the toolkit she's learned during her trauma and addiction recovery, she's mentored and inspired thousands with her vulnerability, authenticity, intuition, and storytelling. Stacy believes that "everything we need to be successful is already within us and we must give ourselves permission to embody all we desire."

**SUZANNE "XENA" LESKO** is a retired U.S. Navy Captain and combat veteran, turned professional speaker and expert advisor. She served for 26 years as a Naval Aviator and then as a Public Affairs Officer. Suzanne graduated from the U.S. Naval Academy, and is one of an elite group of women to reach the rank of Captain in the U.S. Navy ("the 1% of the 1% club"). Suzanne was trained to survive and "return with honor" in intense scenarios at both The Quigley, in Quantico, Virginia and the highest level of the Survival, Evasion, Resistance, and Escape (SERE) program, where she was an instructor. She led and directed large-scale campaigns, missions, operations, and teams in challenging environments around the world, including war zones. And she did it backwards.. in high heels... and Kevlar!

Suzanne is now a sought-after speaker and advisor, operating under her Warrior Advisor™ brand. She leverages her military training, global experience, expertise, and mindset to help leaders and organizations excel in leadership and management, resilience, elite performance, and public affairs. She is also CEO with Multiverse Health (a startup medical device manufacturer),and was previously Federal Partner with Kyndryl (formerly IBM Global Services). She has acted as a specialist advisor and subject matter expert to Grant Thornton, Valiant Integrated Services, and Wharton Leadership Ventures. Suzanne holds a bachelor's degree in Political Science (minor in Spanish), and a master's degree in Global Leadership; she is also a recent graduate of Tuck's Next Step program at Dartmouth.

'Xena' connects with audiences and clients through keynote presentations, panels, podcasts, workshops, executive coaching sessions, and bespoke consulting projects. Suzanne shares stunning stories, hard-won insights, and actionable recommendations via her 'Amazing Tales of The Warrior Advisor' keynote, Resilient Leader Mindset™ program, and Mastery of Optimal Performance workshop. She also acts as an advisor or leader for more complex engagements, such as start-up or non-profit management, public affairs consultancy, operations planning, and go-to-market strategies. Suzanne's sidekick and wingman is Captain Morgen, her water-spilling, paper-chewing Golden Retriever!

**TAMEKA RUSHING** was born and raised in Biloxi, Mississippi, Tameka Rushing's formative years were shaped by her involvement in the Boys and Girls Club and active community service, for which the city recognized her. These early experiences instilled a deep sense of community and leadership in her. Tameka's philosophy, "Unlock the latent potential in emerging managers," reflects her commitment to guiding individuals to become motivational leaders. Her unique blend of military discipline and corporate savvy creates a culture of relentless personal growth and resilience, epitomized by her mantra, "Forming Leaders. Uniting Teams."

Leading Glass Half Full Solutions LLC as its award-winning CEO and the creator of Zesty Reads™, Tameka transforms managers into inspiring leaders. She infuses self-care and growth into everyday life. Her leadership journey is underpinned by over two decades of experience in military and corporate healthcare training. Tameka's effectiveness as a facilitator was lauded by a previous client, Head of ERG Strategy at Amazon, who highlighted her insightful DiSC debrief workshop, praising Tameka's deep understanding of the DiSC model, engaging delivery and ability to connect with the team on a personal level.

Spending 10 of her 21 years in the military overseas has allowed Tameka to work with diverse cultures, enriching her approach to leadership and team building. A respected Air Force veteran, her roles as Commandant and Functional Manager for the military's new leaders have further enriched her leadership ethos. Her authored works on self-discovery and growth mindset, combined with her love for travel, underscore her commitment to continuous personal and professional development. Tameka's approach integrates military discipline with corporate agility, promoting a learning culture and personal growth within her teams and positioning her as an industry leader.

**TAMMY LYNN LAIRD** is a US Army and Air Force (USAF) Veteran, homeschool teacher, former Classical Conversations Challenge Director, Trauma Resiliency Peer Coach for 22ZERO, and children's author. During her Army service, she was a counterintelligence assistant/agent and interrogator in the Reserves. In the USAF, she served as a personnel officer in various roles including as a squadron section commander for both a Civil Engineer squadron and an Aircraft Maintenance squadron. During these years, she took care of her troops, and their families as specific personnel issues arose. As the Chief of Education and Training for the E-3 Sentry Airborne Warning and Control System (AWACS), Laird meticulously oversaw syllabi and curriculum development for all of the crew positions, as well as seeking to improve the quality of the training through interviews and graduate evaluations. She was the lead instructor in training the trainers for these various crew positions. Currently, the focus of her leadership and instruction are centralized at home. She is grateful to be able to homeschool and learn new things alongside her children and has enjoyed serving in various leadership positions within the homeschool community.

Having cared for her peers in the Army (both on active duty and in the Reserves), Laird continued to do so in Air Force ROTC, and later with her troops in the USAF upon commissioning. She has ceaselessly prayed over her brothers and sisters in the military, in all phases and in all branches. It is her hope to end feelings of isolation, lack of purpose, or suffering from invisible traumas and post-traumatic stress (PTS) by reaching out to those in need. She also desires to ease the transition from active duty to civilian life through connection, camaraderie, and community. As a 22ZERO Trauma Resiliency Peer Coach, she has been able to guide veterans, first responders, their immediate family members, and our Gold Star Families to heal from PTS, anxiety, depression, and other negative emotions.

Laird has published two children's books, "Introducing Beatrice," and "Valiant Charlie Defeats the Sleep Monster," and is currently working on other writing endeavors, including a third book for our veterans, first responders and their families, celebrating and telling their story as our heroes. She is known as "Hallmark," "Overwatch," and the "Heart and Soul of Angels14" by her cherished brothers and sisters among various veteran organizations. Laird is a happily married wife, devoted mother, and lives in the Austin, Texas area with her best friend and husband of over 28 years, their sons, and her precious mother.

# DR. TRACEY JONES is a multifaceted individual with a remarkable journey encompassing various roles and experiences. An author, speaker, podcaster, and international leadership expert, she serves as the President of Tremendous Leadership and T3 Solutions. In 2009, she took over from her father, Charlie "Tremendous" Jones, a legend in the insurance and motivational arenas. Tracey's diverse career has spanned top positions across four major industries, including the military, high tech, defense contracting, and publishing.

A graduate of the United States Air Force Academy, Tracey is a decorated veteran who served in both the First Gulf War and the Bosnian War. Her commitment to learning led her to earn an MBA in Global Management and a Ph.D. in Leadership Studies from Lancaster Bible College. She also imparts her knowledge as an adjunct professor for the American College of Financial Services and received an honorary Doctor of Humane Letters from Central Penn College in 2017.

Beyond her professional achievements, Tracey's company has contributed over $4 million to local homeless shelters, recovery outreach and mission groups, disaster recovery organizations, and scholarships to local colleges in the past 15 years. She also conducts monthly book club programs at several Pennsylvania State Correctional Institutions (SCI) and holds the role of Chairperson for The Center for Military and Veterans Affairs of the American College, where she facilitates military members and spouses' transitions into financial services careers. Tracey resides in Enola, PA, with her husband, Mike, and passionately engages in outdoor activities, biking, traveling, writing, publishing, spending time with her rescue pets, and equipping others with the tools to lead a tremendous life.

**TRAVIS MILLS** is a recalibrated warrior, motivational speaker, actor, author and an advocate for veterans and amputees. He retired United States Army Staff Sergeant Travis Mills of the 82nd Airborne. Despite losing portions of both arms and legs from an IED while on active duty in Afghanistan, Travis continues to overcome life's challenges, breaking physical barriers and defying odds. Travis lives by his motto: "Never give up. Never quit."

On April 10, 2012, United States Army Staff Sergeant Travis Mills of the 82nd Airborne was critically injured on his third tour of duty in Afghanistan by an IED (improvised explosive device) while on patrol, losing portions of both legs and both arms. He is one of only five quadruple amputees from the wars in Iraq and Afghanistan to survive his injuries.

Thanks to his amazing strength, courage, an incredible will to live, the heroic actions of the men in his unit, the prayers of thousands, and all the healthcare providers at the Walter Reed Army Medical Center, near Washington D.C., Travis remains on the road to recovery. Every day is a battle, but Travis continues to astound friends and family alike with his progress and with his amazing spirit.

**VALERIE ELLIS LAVIN** is a visionary leader with a remarkable impact in nonprofit, for-profit, and military sectors. Her career showcases a unique combination of leadership, community engagement, and entrepreneurial skills. A key focus of her journey is fostering entrepreneurship among military veterans and their families. As a Co-Founder of Action Zone, INC. in Tampa, FL, Valerie played a crucial role in establishing the first-ever nonprofit to secure a contract with Veterans Florida's Entrepreneurship Training, securing substantial funds.

Valerie's influence extends to her roles on the Disabled American Veterans National Veterans Entrepreneurship Council and as a former Director of Ecosystem Development and Ambassador Program at Bunker Labs. Through her strategic guidance and leadership, 38 volunteer Ambassadors and their communities have thrived, inspiring, equipping, and connecting veteran and military spouse entrepreneurs, fostering entrepreneurial growth and collaboration. As CEO and Founder of Luminary Global, Valerie has solidified her reputation as a dynamic business leader, earning recognition as Business Woman of the Year finalist twice and Tampa Bay Business and Wealth Magazine, Apogee Award winner.

With a distinguished 21-year military background in the U.S. Army, Valerie has made significant contributions to national strategic objectives, earning prestigious awards such as the Bronze Star Medal and Defense Meritorious Service Medal. Her outstanding community involvement, marked by accolades like the Veterans of Foreign Affairs #StillServing Honoree and the Gasparilla Community Hero Award, underscores her dedication. Valerie's transformative impact across business, military advocacy, and community engagement positions her as a dynamic force for change and empowerment.

**VIAN MORALES** is a Veteran Army Officer, creative Operations Strategist, The Citadel's 33rd Black Female graduate and a breathwork facilitator. She currently serves as the SVP of Operations at Beckley Retreats and is fiercely passionate about sharing the science-backed benefits and ancient wisdom of psychedelics. Vian has dedicated herself to bringing safe wellbeing experiences to a larger audience, especially making holistic health more accessible to veterans and the BIPOC community.

Growing up in a very active family in Macon, GA, Vian discovered the importance of physical health at a young age. As a Division I soccer player, she learned to manage her health challenges to become a top performer. With nearly two decades of managing people and processes in the corporate sector, Vian quickly recognized the burnout and mental health issues surrounding her. She found it challenging to access science-based, safe, holistic options especially supportive of the BIPOC community. After continuously experiencing the devastation of witnessing soldiers and friends battle mental health issues, losing many of them to suicide, Vian entered into a journey of deep internal work, re-grounding herself through yoga, meditation, breathwork, and sound healing. Ultimately, she dedicated herself and made it her mission to use her skillset in service, building community and helping others tap into ancient wisdom and experience the transformative power of wellness-based therapies and psychedelics.

She is particularly passionate about making holistic health more accessible to veterans, the BIPOC community as well as those who suffer from chronic conditions. Lived experience combined with creative business acumen have driven and informed Vian in her mission to create meaningful change and expand opportunities for deep healing to people around the world, focused especially on those communities who have historically been left behind.

**VICTORIA RYDIN BONCZ** is a retired Chief Master Sergeant with a remarkable career spanning more than 26 years in the United States Air Force. Throughout the majority of her career, she was a journalist and communication professional within Public Affairs.

Hailing from humble beginnings in a small town in northern Illinois, Victoria began her military journey immediately after high school, propelling herself into an unknown world of unique and challenging opportunities. Traversing the globe, she navigated diplomatic circles, engaging with foreign royalty and negotiating with representatives of socialist governments. She contributed to the construction of schools and water pump stations in remote Indo-Pacific islands; played a pivotal role in disaster response efforts, assisting in rescue and recovery activities in the aftermath of hurricanes and earthquakes.

Prior to her retirement, Victoria had the honor of serving as the Senior Enlisted Leader for Public Affairs at Air Force Special Operations Command at Hurlburt Field, Florida. Here she served as a communication strategist and trusted advisor to the commander, command chief, and staff.

Post-retirement, Victoria traded her high-paced, high-stress military life for a year of introspection, personal growth, and travel with friends and family. Presently, she is channeling her energy into building her portfolio as a real estate investor and growing her pet care business. Additionally, Victoria is actively involved in facilitating courses on personal and professional development, keen on helping individuals and teams transform their mindsets, break free from limiting narratives, and embrace their true value to achieve their dreams.

# ACKNOWLEDGEMENTS

It takes a village to write a book like this. Many thanks to:

*Alex Fredericks, Amanda Catarzi, Amobi Okugo, Bridgette Bello, Dave Sanderson, David Homan, Diane Byrne, Elizabeth Marion, Garth Massey, Garrett Klugh, Gene Moran, J Scot Heathman, Jason Ford, Jeff Turk, Kirsten Brunson, Laura Noel, Michael Beas, Mike Sarraille, Molly Jenks, Phil Randazzo, Rachelle Fender, Raymond Jackson, Rob Vaka, Ruben Gonzalez, Sal Filardi, Scott Garber, Scott MacGregor, Stacy Raske & Suzanne Lesko*

# ABOUT THE AUTHOR

## IT'S PERSONAL

Born & raised on the coast of Maine, life was idealic, and all one could hope for. But the cold winters were not to my liking, and I ran off to Florida for college, thinking I never would return. A few years after the birth of my daughter I returned to the Pine Tree State. It's where my ex-wife grew up, and where our child would be raised.

Yarmouth, Maine became my new home. It was there I was blessed beyond measure, becoming a youth sports coach in soccer & softball. Being beside my daughter till her last high school game on the softball field is a memory I will cherish for the rest of my life.

My first trip to Costa Rica was in 2017. I fell in love at first. The country is beautiful beyond description, and its people are some of the nicest I have ever met. Now I travel there 3-4 times a year and am involved in a number of projects to support local job creation, protect the environment, and strengthen new relationships. Pura vida!

*Some fun facts about me:*

Avid pickleball player (yes, I'm one of those)

Baseball Card Collector, still holding on to 200 precious pieces from the late 70's.

Closet Poet, having written hundreds of short ones over the years.

Hopeless Romantic. Who isn't? Still searching for my other half.

Once a "decent" dancer of Bachata & Salsa. Need to get back on the floor!

1st Degree Black belt in Tae Kwon Do

## THE BUSINESS

Storyteller, Disruptor, Sherpa of Business Relationships

My business path has been full of the usual ups and downs. I often tell people I sold everything but used cars and vacuum cleaners (came close though, as I worked for a rental car agency and "sold" time shares on Daytona Beach).

Networking became part of my life in 1994, joining a BNI group. Since then, I have written hundreds of articles on the subject, consulted Chambers of Commerce, and launched four private business networks (from local to a global private organization). In the spring of '23 I released my first book called The Network Effect(www.thenetworkeffect.ai)

It's an honor to bring together amazing executives from around the world. My networks have included professional athletes & teams, entertainers, and business executives from every vertical (and almost every country) in the world. Since 2004, I have hosted countless networking events, Panel Discussions, Red Carpet parties, and VIP Dinners.

Now I have a new family, a new community, and new causes to get involved in. The *Military Effect* has been a blessing in disguise. There is much work to do, and I couldn't be more excited about what lies ahead. It's my turn to serve!

Made in the USA
Middletown, DE
27 May 2024